Christianizing
the WORLD

David J. Engelsma

Christianizing
the WORLD

Reformed Calling or Ecclesiastical Suicide?

REFORMED
FREE PUBLISHING
ASSOCIATION

Scripture cited is taken from the King James (Authorized) Version

Reformed Free Publishing Association
1894 Georgetown Center Drive
Jenison, MI 49428
(616) 457-5970
www.rfpa.org
mail@rfpa.org

Cover and interior design by Erika Kiel

ISBN 978-1-944555-02-3
Ebook ISBN 978-1-944555-03-0
LCCN 2016936929

To Ruth

CONTENTS

PREFACE

For many years, it has been widely accepted in Reformed circles worldwide that the theory of common grace developed by the Dutch theologian Abraham Kuyper and the project of Christianizing the world by this common grace, which Kuyper exhorted, are Reformed orthodoxy. Of late, this thinking spreads among evangelicals both in North America and across the world.

In the past few years, the Kuyperian dream (others would say "vision") has captivated Reformed, Presbyterian, and evangelical scholars and institutions to the extent that they have made common cause with the Acton Institute, the essentially Roman Catholic organization in Grand Rapids, Michigan, to translate Kuyper's three massive volumes on common grace from the original Dutch into English. The practical purpose of this scholarly enterprise is the Christianizing of North America and eventually the whole world.

Few, if any, question this quixotic (ad)venture with regard to its biblical and Reformed bases. Conservative and liberal Reformed theologians, scholars, churches, and seminaries alike enthusiastically endorse and promote the project and its theological foundation and source in a common grace of God.

This book examines the theory of common grace and its cultural ambitions in light of the Reformed creeds and holy scripture, particularly the passages of scripture to which Kuyper and his disciples mainly appeal. The book also calls attention to the deleterious effects of the theory of common grace upon the churches and schools that have adopted it and put it into practice. These well-known and prestigious institutions include the Reformed Churches in the Netherlands, the Free University of Amsterdam, the Christian Reformed Church in North America, and Calvin College in Grand Rapids, Michigan.

The conclusion, which one who honestly confronts the evidence can hardly deny, is that the emperor has no clothes. As a purportedly Reformed doctrine—indeed to hear its advocates it is one of the chief Reformed doctrines (rejection of which warrants exclusion from the Reformed community)— the theory of common grace has no parentage in the Reformed faith of scripture and the creeds. As a supposedly Reformed calling, Christianizing the world of the ungodly is not the legitimate offspring of Reformed Christianity.

The first and main part of the book is a much-expanded version of a public lecture given in Grand Rapids, Michigan, in 2014 under the auspices of the evangelism society of Southwest Protestant Reformed Church in Wyoming, Michigan. An important part of the expansion is the inclusion in the book of quotations and other references, with accompanying footnotes, which substantiate the book's analysis and critique. In a lecture, such material becomes tedious. In a book of this nature, they are necessary.

The second part of the book consists of questions raised by the audience at the conclusion of the lecture and of the answers by the speaker at the lecture (also the author of the book). Coming as they did from some who were hostile to the content of the lecture, as well as from others who, although supporters of the thesis of the speech, nevertheless desired more information or proof, these questions with the answers make for interesting reading.

The title of the book was shortened in keeping with contemporary conventions, if not so that it would fit on the cover. Originally, the title was *Abraham Kuyper's Common Grace Christianizing of Culture—Reformed Calling or Ecclesiastical Suicide?* Regardless of the title on the cover, this is the book's content.

INTRODUCTION TO PART 1

This book has both an immediate occasion and a deep background.

The immediate occasion is the ongoing translation and publication in English, for the first time, of the three volumes on common grace by Dutch Reformed theologian and politician Abraham Kuyper (1837–1920).[1] Significantly, the project of publishing Kuyper's work on common grace is the cooperative effort of prominent Reformed theologians and churchmen and of the Acton Institute. The Acton Institute is a think tank that is heavily influenced by Roman Catholic theologians and therefore by the Roman Catholic Church. The co-founder and president of the Acton Institute is the Roman Catholic priest Robert A. Sirico. This cooperation of Reformed and Roman Catholic theologians and agencies is significant because Kuyper's theory of common grace was intended by Kuyper to advance the alliance of Reformed and Roman Catholics in the Netherlands on behalf of his effort to Christianize the Netherlands and to propel himself into a position of political power.

The project of translating and publishing Kuyper's books on common grace in English has an important spiritual, social, and practical purpose: the Christianizing of the culture of North America and eventually of the whole world.

---

1 Abraham Kuyper, *De Gemeene Gratie* [Common Grace] (Amsterdam: Hoveker & Wormser, 1902–4). Volume 1 is subtitled, in English translation, *The Historical Part*; volume 2, *The Doctrinal Part*; and volume 3, *The Practical Part*. The intention is to publish Kuyper's original, three-volume work in nine volumes of English translation. The first three volumes of this projected series are now available. All quotations from that part of Kuyper's work that has already been translated are taken from these volumes. Quotations taken from those parts of Kuyper's *Common Grace* that remain untranslated are my translations of the Dutch original.

The opening paragraphs of the first volume of the English translation describe the program behind the translation project as "social reform" and "cultural engagement."[2] The project is a sortie in the culture wars.

The source, the dynamic power, and the defense of this contemporary campaign by Rome and an odd alliance of evangelicals and Reformed thinkers to Christianize the world is Kuyper's theory of common grace, which Kuyper proposed and developed most fully in his three large volumes titled *Common Grace.*

Deep Background

If this current project of translation and of the contemporary campaign to Christianize America and then the world are the immediate occasion of the present book, the deep background is threefold. First, in the early twentieth century, when Kuyper wrote his monumental work on common grace, the Reformed Churches in the Netherlands—Kuyper's denomination of churches—bought into Kuyper's theory of common grace and its cultural calling to Christianize the Netherlands and then the world. Kuyper, himself a virtually irresistible force in his churches, was aided in promoting the common grace program by his able, influential colleague Herman Bavinck. Although I will mostly mention and reference Kuyper in this book, I recognize that the highly esteemed Bavinck defended and promoted the common grace Christianizing of culture as enthusiastically and resolutely as did Kuyper.[3]

The Kuyper/Bavinck project of the early twentieth century is simply being replicated today, some one hundred years later, by their theological disciples and by institutions influenced by Kuyper and Bavinck. This replication includes cooperation

---

2   Abraham Kuyper, *Common Grace: Noah–Adam*, trans. Nelson D. Kloosterman and Ed M. van der Maas, ed. Jordan J. Ballor and Stephen J. Grabill (Grand Rapids, MI: Christian's Library Press [Acton Institute], 2013), xi.

3   Cf. Herman Bavinck, "Common Grace," trans. Raymond C. Van Leeuwen, *Calvin Theological Journal* 24, no. 1 (April 1989): 38–65. This article was originally Bavinck's rectoral address at Kampen in December 1894. The Dutch title was *"De Gemeene Genade."*

in the Christianizing enterprise by Calvinists and Roman Catholics. In Kuyper's day, it was the cooperation of Kuyper, his Reformed Churches in the Netherlands, and Kuyper's Free University with the Roman Catholic priest and politician Herman Schaepman, Schaepman's Roman Catholic political party, and to some extent the Roman Catholic Church. Today it is the cooperation of Reformed theologian Nelson Kloosterman and other Reformed theologians of the Abraham Kuyper Translation Society, Calvin College, Fuller Theological Seminary, Kuyper College, Dordt College, and Mid-America Reformed Seminary with the Acton Institute, which involves Roman Catholic theologians and necessarily, in view of the hierarchy of Rome, the Roman Catholic Church.

Therefore, we are warranted in asking the question, how did the Kuyper/Bavinck project of Christianizing the Netherlands in the early 1900s and subsequent years turn out? What were the effects on the Netherlands? Has that small country, with its sizable population of Reformed church members, been Christianized?

Yes, and what have been the effects of the Christianizing project on the Reformed Churches in the Netherlands? On the Free University of Amsterdam? On the theology and theologians influenced by Kuyper's cultural common grace? Are they all still soundly Reformed? Are they even Christian? Or has the Kuyperian Christianizing program actually turned out to be ecclesiastical suicide?

With these questions, the contemporary advocates of Kuyper's theory of the common grace Christianizing of culture do not concern themselves. About these questions, they are all studiously silent. To the obvious historical realities raised by these questions, they are blind.

But this is the first aspect of the deep background of the contemporary development regarding common grace that occasions this book: what has Kuyper's theory of common grace accomplished in his country and society, and what has the effect of the theory been on the churches and other institutions that embraced it?

A second aspect of the deep background is the repudiation of the entire common grace theory and its cultural program in the early 1920s by the young Christian Reformed preacher and theologian Herman Hoeksema. By synodical decision, in 1924 the Christian Reformed Church in North America adopted, and thus fully committed itself to, Kuyper's theory of common grace and its cultural, Christianizing purpose. The Christian Reformed Church made this decision in its adoption of the three points of common grace as binding church dogma. This dogma affirms that God is gracious to all humans without exception; that in this grace God restrains sin in all humans; and that by virtue of this common grace of God all humans are able to perform good works in the sphere of civil society.[4]

The fundamental doctrine expressed by the three points of common grace is that there is an important work of the grace of God in history that consists of making a society and eventually all the world Christian. As a work of the very grace of God in both unregenerated unbelievers and regenerated believers, this cultural work of God permits, indeed requires, the cooperation of Christians with the ungodly.

Having adopted this doctrine of common grace, at once the Christian Reformed Church disciplined Hoeksema for his public condemnation of the doctrine of common grace and its purported power of Christianizing American society. This was the origin of the Protestant Reformed Churches in America as a distinct denomination of Reformed churches.

Both before and after the common grace decision of 1924, Hoeksema called the attention of the Christian Reformed Church and of the watching Reformed community of churches to the fact that the Reformed creeds teach absolutely

---

4   For the three points of common grace as adopted by the Christian Reformed Church in 1924, in the original Dutch language, see the *Acta der Synode 1924 van de Christelijke Gereformeerde Kerk* [*Acts of Synod 1924 of the Christian Reformed Church*], 18 June to 8 July, 1924, held in Kalamazoo, Michigan, 145–47. For the three points in English translation, see Herman Hoeksema, *The Protestant Reformed Churches in America: Their Origin, Early History and Doctrine*, 2nd ed. (Grand Rapids, MI, 1947), 84–86.

nothing about the supposedly fundamental doctrine of common grace, with its purpose and power of Christianizing the world. In addition, he warned that the doctrine, with its resulting practice, would make the churches that adopted the doctrine and practiced its teaching thoroughly worldly. That is, he warned that the adoption of the doctrine of common grace would prove to be ecclesiastical suicide.

This warning the Protestant Reformed Churches have continued to give right up to the present time, which renders these churches as unpopular with the Reformed community of churches as the prophets of the Old Testament were with national Israel.

With the sole exception of a brief notice of Hoeksema's objection to the theory of common grace in a footnote in Richard J. Mouw's introduction to the translated volumes of Kuyper's work on common grace—for which Mouw is to be praised, not only for doing full justice to the history of the adoption of the doctrine of common grace by the Christian Reformed Church, but also for indicating, no matter how faintly, a warning against the virtually uncritical acceptance of the theory by the Reformed community—the architects and advocates of the current common grace project completely ignore Hoeksema and his reasoned arguments and accurate warnings against common grace and its cultural pretensions.[5]

How strange! How strange this silence on the part of the Christian Reformed participants in this project and of their common grace allies regarding the voice of one who, at the time being one of their own and one known as an ardent disciple of Kuyper in all respects other than Kuyper's theory of common grace, said no. It is as though, after the flood, a learned group formed with the express purpose of repeating

---

5 Having referred to "the opponents of Kuyper's common grace theology within the Reformed tradition," Mouw, in a footnote, instances "Herman Hoeksema." Mouw refers the readers to Hoeksema's history of the Protestant Reformed Churches in America for "the texts of numerous documents dealing with debates about common grace in the Dutch Calvinist community, as well as his own extensive case against Kuyper's theology" (Richard J. Mouw, "Kuyper on Common Grace," in Kuyper, *Common Grace: Noah–Adam*, xxvi).

all the conditions on account of which the flood came and never mentioned Noah or his hundred-year warnings.

This aspect of the deep background of the contemporary venture concerning common grace makes the venture a matter of interest and, still more, of responsibility to the Protestant Reformed Churches. No other churches will, or are able to, expose the contemporary venture of Christianizing the world on the advice of Kuyper and by the power of Kuyper's common grace.

The third aspect of the deep background of the contemporary promotion of common grace and its cultural workings, as of this book, is less well known than the preceding two. This aspect concerns the background of Kuyper and Bavinck's own attraction to and promotion of the theory of common grace as a Christianizing influence on worldly culture. It concerns the theological thinking in Europe at the time that Kuyper and Bavinck produced their doctrine of common grace, indeed the theological thinking for some two hundred years prior to Kuyper and Bavinck. Out of this essentially modernist, that is, unbelieving, thinking rose the Kuyperian doctrine of common grace, which was then made binding dogma in the Christian Reformed Church by its common grace decisions of 1924. To this I return later, in my criticism of the common grace project.

Nature of the Book

In this book, I concern myself strictly, or almost strictly, as strictly as is possible, with Kuyper's theory of common grace *as a cultural doctrine*; as a teaching that accounts for the supposed doing of good, in the judgment of God, by unbelievers in the sphere of civil society; as a teaching that calls Christians to unite with non-Christians in making America and the world Christian. My subject therefore is those elements of the three points of common grace adopted by the Christian Reformed Church in 1924, and widely accepted by the broader Reformed and Presbyterian community of churches, that consist of a favor, or grace, of God to the ungodly in everyday, natural life; of a restraint of sin in the unregenerate, so that they are not totally depraved, as otherwise they would be; and of the ability of the unbeliever, by this grace of God, to perform truly good works in the sphere of civil and cultural activities. The subject is the notion of a Christianizing of the world by a common grace of God that unites believer and unbeliever in the noble project.

In keeping with G. K. Chesterton's dictum that "any one setting out to dispute anything ought always to begin by saying what he does not dispute. Beyond stating what he proposes to prove he should always state what he does not propose to prove," I make clear at the outset what I do not intend to prove.[6] I do not intend to prove that common grace always involves, or inevitably leads to, the heresy of universalizing the saving grace of God and therefore to the doctrine that the saving grace of God is resistible, dependent for its efficacy on the will of the sinner. This, I firmly believe.

The history of the Christian Reformed Church convincingly demonstrates this. Intending to affirm Kuyper's doctrine of a cultural common grace, the Christian Reformed synod of 1924 adopted as official church dogma the doctrine that God has a gracious desire for the salvation of all humans without exception. This is the teaching in the first point of common grace that God's grace toward all humans is expressed in a "general offer of the gospel."[7] A grace expressed in an "offer of the gospel" is a (would-be) *saving* grace. A saving grace expressed in a "general offer" is a saving grace that fails to save many to whom God extends it and is thus identified as the universal,

---

6   G. K. Chesterton, *Orthodoxy* (Wheaton, IL: Harold Shaw, 1994), 5.

7   For the Dutch original, see the *Acta der Synode 1924 van de Christelijke Gereformeerde Kerk*, 146. The Dutch speaks of *"de algemeene aanbieding des Evangelies"* as the expression of *"een zekere gunst of genade Gods."* The English translation is found in Hoeksema's *Protestant Reformed Churches in America*: "a certain favor or grace of God [expressed in]...the general offer of the gospel" (85).

resistible grace of Arminianism, which the Reformed faith condemns and repudiates in the Canons of Dordt.[8]

This I have argued in a book demonstrating that the Christian Reformed adoption in 1924 of a common grace of God has produced in that church the doctrine of universal atonement in the 1960s and the open denial of predestination in the late 1970s and early 1980s.[9]

But Kuyper contended that his common grace was essentially different from Arminianism's universal, saving grace and that it must not be confused with Arminianism's theology of universal, resistible grace. Therefore, I refrain in this book from charging his theory of common grace with inevitably opening the way in Reformed churches that embrace his teaching to the doctrine of universal, ineffectual saving grace.

I examine Kuyper's theory of a common grace of God that intends the Christianizing of the culture, or way of earthly life, of the world outside the church. The question I will answer is whether such Christianizing of the world by a common grace of God is the calling of Reformed Christians, as Kuyper urged, or ecclesiastical suicide.

---

8 Canons of Dordt 3-4.10-14, Canons of Dordt 2.8, in Philip Schaff, ed., *The Creeds of Christendom with a History and Critical Notes*, 6th ed., 3 vols. (New York: Harper and Row, 1931; repr., Grand Rapids, MI: Baker Books, 2007), 3:589-91, 587. See also Canons 3-4.4, errors 1-9, in *The Confessions and the Church Order of the Protestant Reformed Churches* (Grandville, MI: Protestant Reformed Churches in America, 2005), 167, 170-73. Schaff does not include the rejection of errors of the Canons in English translation.

9 See David J. Engelsma, *Hyper-Calvinism and the Call of the Gospel: An Examination of the Well-Meant Offer of the Gospel*, 3rd ed. (Jenison, MI: Reformed Free Publishing Association, 2014).

CHAPTER 1

The Kuyperian Common Grace Project

Let us first be clear as to what Kuyper and Bavinck and their theological and ecclesiastical allies and disciples had as the purpose or goal of their theory of common grace in the early twentieth century in the Netherlands. This is also the purpose of Kuyper's disciples in North America today with their translation of Kuyper's books on common grace and their promotion of the theology of common grace.

Kuyper wanted to influence the culture of his day. His elaborate theory of common grace was a cultural doctrine, in the service of a cultural project. By "culture," we should understand the earthly way of life of a nation, including not only morals, but also science, the arts, government, education, and family life. Roughly, by culture is meant what we have in mind by "everyday, earthly life in the world." In the theory of common grace, culture refers to all of life, apart from church life; all of life excepting public worship, doctrinal confession of the truth, prayer, and related spiritual activities.

Kuyper was convinced that the Reformed people in the Netherlands slighted culture and the cultural calling they shared with all Netherlanders. Indeed, he feared that the Dutch Reformed people of his day spurned culture and rejected the cultural calling altogether. Kuyper's code word for this perceived evil was "Anabaptism," with reference to certain Baptists in the time of the Reformation who withdrew physically from earthly society and tried to live in physical separation from the ungodly world. These Baptists cared only for the spiritual condition of their souls, or so they said. Not inaccurately, the Dutch Reformed adversaries of this conception of the Christian life summed up the thinking of these Baptists regarding the Christian life thus: *"met een boekje in een hoekje"* ("with a little [religious] book in a little corner").

Kuyper charged that many Reformed believers restricted their calling as Christians to a good, active church life, ignoring and even repudiating an equally vigorous Christian life in society and in all areas of human culture.

Christianizing the Culture

Kuyper wanted to influence the culture in such an effective way as to make the culture "Christian." He and Bavinck coined the term for this activity: "Christianizing" (the culture). Bavinck wrote, "We have to aim at that mighty, glorious, rich ideal to *Christianize* the world."[1] He immediately added that this Christianizing of the world must be done "by bringing in our Reformed confession into all areas of life." The modern Reformed advocates of the Christianizing project conveniently ignore this role of the Reformed confession in Christianizing the world. The Reformed confession is a hindrance to their cultural mission. The Reformed confession would certainly not promote cooperation between Calvinism and the Roman Catholicism of the Acton Institute.

By the Christianizing of the world, Kuyper and Bavinck did not mean that the life of a nation and ultimately of the entire world becomes truly Christian, that is, a life lived by at least a majority of humans who are born again by the Holy Spirit and believers in Jesus Christ. They did not have in

---

1 Cited in Willem J. de Wit, *On the Way to the Living God: A Cathartic Reading of Herman Bavinck and an Invitation to Overcome the Plausibility Crisis of Christianity* (Amsterdam: VU University Press, 2011), 58; emphasis added.

mind a life of love for God and the neighbor from the heart, in accordance with the ten commandments of the law of God, even though this is the only life that is truly Christian. Not at all!

Kuyper was well aware that the majority of the citizens of the Netherlands were, and would always be, unregenerated, unsaved unbelievers, who did not love God nor keep the commandments out of love for God. But by Christianizing the culture of a nation, Kuyper meant a certain influence of Christianity on the culture, so that outwardly the everyday, earthly life of the citizens conformed somewhat to Christian standards. This external conformity to Christian standards could be described as Christian because the citizens, even though mostly unbelievers, had a certain regard for and delight in Christianity and its way of life.

On this crucial point, Kuyper himself must speak.

> "Christian" [in the phrase "Christianizing the nation"] therefore says nothing about the spiritual state of the inhabitants of such a country but only witnesses to the fact that public opinion, the general mind-set, the ruling ideas, the moral norms, the laws and customs there clearly betoken the influence of the Christian faith.[2]

According to Kuyper, therefore, a Christianized nation is a society and nation that still lie in the darkness of idolatry, unbelief, and unrighteousness, but that have become more decent, moral, and orderly.

Remains of the Image of God

One might conclude that a Christianized nation in Kuyper's thinking is one upon which a veneer of Christianity has been applied, were it not that Kuyper taught that Christianizing a nation also consists of a certain *inner* work of grace that improves the ungodly inhabitants of a nation and its ungodly

---

2   Abraham Kuyper, "Common Grace," in *Abraham Kuyper: A Centennial Reader*, ed. James D. Bratt (Grand Rapids, MI: Eerdmans, 1998), 199.

society *spiritually.* Especially does Kuyper plainly teach that common grace is a working of God within the ungodly that retains some real good, indeed part of the image of God in which man was created, in the unregenerated, depraved sinner. This account of his common grace appears especially in Kuyper's defense of common grace as a restraint of sin. This aspect of his doctrine of common grace makes common cause with the semi-Pelagian and Arminian error of the denial of total depravity and opens up his theory, indeed in history *did in fact* open up his theory, to the rank Arminian heresy of universal, ineffectual, *saving* grace.

According to Kuyper, common grace is more than "an external coercive force." On the contrary,

> from within us it restrains the continued effect and the penetration of the poison of sin, so that it does not rob our whole life, all our inclinations, and all our capacities of all that God's image had imprinted on them...Common grace chose its base within our own heart for its outward working. Thus the small sparks [of the original image of God in man] still glow within us, small remnants are still noticeable there, and that is what common grace makes use of to restrain the madness of sin within us.[3]

Through common grace, "some embers [of man's original righteousness] continued to glow, and small remnants of that original goodness were spared."[4] Apart from common grace, the fall of Adam would have resulted in the spiritual condition of total depravity. But "*common grace* intervened, and...through this common grace of God, sin was prevented

---

3   Abraham Kuyper, *Common Grace: Temptation–Babel*, trans. Nelson D. Kloosterman and Ed M. van der Maas, ed. Jordan J. Ballor and Stephen J. Grabill (Grand Rapids, MI: Christian's Library Press [Acton Institute], 2014), 320. Bavinck agreed: "Traces of the image of God continue in mankind." The result is that "in the things which appertain to this earthly life, [fallen] man can still accomplish much good" (Bavinck, "Common Grace," 51).

4   Abraham Kuyper, *Common Grace: Abraham–Parousia*, trans. Nelson D. Kloosterman and Ed M. van der Maas, ed. Jordan J. Ballor and Stephen J. Grabill (Grand Rapids, MI: Christian's Library Press [Acton Institute], 2014), 609.

from immediately bringing its poisonous, deadly work to full completion" [that is, to the condition of total depravity].[5]

As Kuyper himself observes, the implication of this doctrine of a common grace of God, indeed the purpose of it, is exactly the same as the semi-Pelagian heresy. The natural man, the unsaved world outside of Jesus Christ, is not totally depraved but retains some good—some *real* good, the very good in which God created Adam originally. Fallen humanity is not totally depraved. By this remaining good in itself, fallen, unregenerated, unbelieving humanity is able to perform the very good work of Christianizing society and ultimately the world.

The only difference between semi-Pelagianism and Kuyper's theory of common grace is that semi-Pelagianism attributes the good that remains in fallen man to the limitation of the fall itself. The fall did not effect the total depravity of the sinner, merely a partial depravity. For Kuyperian common grace, the good that remains in all humans is due to the gift of a common grace of God. The effect is the same: the natural man is not totally depraved. He is yet somewhat good and is able therefore to do what is good in the sphere of earthly, everyday life. Ominously, this goodness of the ungodly, unbelieving world is the possibility, if not the necessity, of fellowship with the world on the part of Reformed, believing Christians, especially on behalf of cooperation with the world in Christianizing the world.

Kuyper himself acknowledges the essential similarity of his theory of common grace and of semi-Pelagianism, although his purpose is to promote his theory as a defense against semi-Pelagianism.

> The doctrine of original sin, i.e., of the *total* depravity of our human nature, is again and again in danger of being weakened in a semi-Pelagian sense whenever we attempt to explain these "small traces" [of alleged remnants of the

---

5   Kuyper, *Common Grace: Temptation–Babel*, 312; emphasis is Kuyper's.

image of God in fallen humans] on the basis of anything other than "common grace."[6]

Both semi-Pelagianism and Kuyperian common grace deny that the fallen, natural man is totally depraved. Both doctrines affirm some remaining good in the unsaved sinner. Both proclaim that fallen mankind, outside of Jesus Christ, is able to accomplish great things with its remaining goodness. What distinguishes Kuyper's view of the fallen race from the view of semi-Pelagianism is that Kuyper attributes the goodness of the natural man to common grace.

Another difference concerns the purposes of the semi-Pelagians and of Kuyper. Semi-Pelagianism wanted, and in its modern representatives still wants, to ascribe to the sinner a decisive role in his own salvation. Kuyper wanted to find in the ungodly world some capability for the forming of good culture, indeed for the Christianizing of the world, although in spite of his intentions, he also opened the way among his Reformed disciples to the semi-Pelagian doctrine of salvation. It was this zeal of "father Abraham [Kuyper]" for the Christianizing of society, the nation, and finally the world that moved the Christian Reformed Church to adopt its three points of common grace, although, like Kuyper, with the theory of a cultural grace of God toward and in all humans, they also adopted the semi-Pelagian and Arminian doctrine of universal, ineffectual, *saving* grace (the well-meant offer).

The zeal for Christianizing the world is alive and well in the Christian Reformed Church still today. In his August 2014 communication to alumni of Calvin College, the college of the Christian Reformed Church in Grand Rapids, Michigan, President Michael K. Le Roy held before the alumni the calling and prospect of the "transformational work of renewing this broken world."[7]

---

6   Ibid., 320.

7   Michael K. Le Roy, "This Square Inch: Updates from Calvin College President Michael K. Le Roy" (August 2014). The missive is not paginated.

This is the mission of Calvin College, in keeping with the common grace decisions of the Christian Reformed Church in 1924. This is the Kuyperian project of the alliance of Reformed theologians and the Acton Institute today.

To be noted in President Le Roy's call for a modern transformational crusade on the part of Reformed Christians is that the goal of the crusade is nothing less than "the world"—not Grand Rapids, Michigan, not the United States, not North America, not Amsterdam, not the Netherlands, but the entire, vast world.

CHAPTER 2

The Power
of Christianizing
the World

It must be evident to all who are not out of their mind that the project of Christianizing North America, to say nothing of the whole world, in 2016 is a gigantic project. Putting Humpty Dumpty together again cannot hold a candle to President Le Roy's project of putting together again our "broken world."

This is not only because the vast majority of citizens are obviously hardened in anti-Christianity, developed in hatred for Jesus Christ and his godly kingdom and opposed to everything that even faintly resembles Christianity and Christianity's holy way of life. Think only of reforming and renewing the sexual culture of the United States, now having legitimized sodomy and lesbianism as a form of holy matrimony by decision of the Supreme Court of the land. A culture, a well-educated culture, decrees and practices such unnatural abomination only if it is being blinded and hardened by the curse of God according to his awful wrath—the very opposite of the common grace fantasy (see Rom. 1:18–32).

But the Christianizing project is huge also because, as Paul writes, Satan is "the god of this world" (2 Cor. 4:4), and as John writes, "the whole world lieth in wickedness" (1 John 5:19).

The world is not merely "broken." It is in bondage to the devil and depraved. This spiritual death is the righteous judgment of God upon a world that has rebelled against him. Movements and masses of optimistic people cannot simply "fix" the world. The need of the world of the ungodly is deliverance from total depravity, from spiritual death. The need of the world of ungodly mankind is not a repair job. Its need is renewal, resurrection from spiritual death. The agent of this resurrection is the Spirit of the risen Jesus Christ, who alone has, indeed *is*, the almighty power of the risen Jesus, applying the resurrection life of Jesus. Such deliverance begins with redemption—redemption by the atoning death of the Son of God in human flesh, obtaining the right with God for a world that is not simply in the condition of death but that is under the sentence of death.

Common, Cultural Grace

Given Kuyper's and his disciples' ambitious project, in the face of the condition of the world and of its overlord—nothing less than making this wicked, Satan-dominated world Christian—we must appreciate Kuyper's affirmation that only a grace of God can accomplish the project. Mere human goodwill and effort cannot Christianize the world. Not even the cooperation of two mighty religious forces, Calvinism and the Roman Catholic Church, can Christianize the world.

Only the grace of God could conceivably Christianize the world—grace, which is always both God's favor, or love, toward a certain object and God's power at work to bless and do good to that object that is loved by God. Indeed, since according to orthodox Christian theology God *is* his perfections, the grace of God is *God* himself in his favor and power. According to Kuyper and his disciples within and without Reformed churches, God himself is at work Christianizing the world, out of an attitude of love and by his divine power.

This Christianizing attitude and power are the common grace of God. The possibility and power of Christianizing the world, according to Kuyper and his contemporary disciples, is a common grace of God.

But what is the common grace of God, which supposedly intends and which also accomplishes (unless this grace proves to be a failure, an inefficacious grace of God, which has a strange sound) the miraculous Christianizing of the world?

Let us be clear: Common grace is a grace of God! It is divine. It is nothing other, and nothing less, than the loving and almighty being of God in a particular revelation of this being as he is engaged in a certain extremely important work in history.

But this grace is common. It is different from the special, particular grace of God that saves sinners from their sin and death and that causes them to live a holy life, out of grateful love to the God who saved, and saves, them in Jesus Christ by the Spirit of the crucified and risen Savior. Common grace is God in a different revelation of himself than his revelation in Jesus Christ in holy scripture. God's revelation of himself in Jesus Christ is the making known of saving grace. And all scripture is the revelation of God in Jesus Christ, as Jesus himself said in John 5:39: "They [the scriptures] are they which testify of me."[1]

How Kuyper hammered on the point that common grace differs, essentially, from particular, saving grace! How Kuyper warned against the confusing of the two graces, with the result that common grace would morph, in the thinking of Reformed churches and people, into the universal,

---

1   Since all scripture is the revelation of Jesus Christ and therefore of the special, saving grace of God, the devotees of Kuyperian common grace must look elsewhere for their knowledge of common grace than to scripture. And they do. They look to the revelation of common grace in the writings of Kuyper, especially the three volumes now being translated into English. These constitute the "Bible" of common grace and its Christianizing mission. I remind the advocates of common grace that Kuyper's volumes are not "given by inspiration of God" and therefore are not "profitable for doctrine" (2 Tim. 3:16), regardless of the zeal in the Reformed community for their teaching. Scripture and the Reformed confessions must be allowed to stand in judgment on Kuyper's theory of common grace. The proponents of common grace and its mission must face the question, "What is the source and basis of the doctrine and mission, keeping in mind that scripture is the message of particular (saving) grace in Jesus Christ, as Jesus himself testified in John 5:39?"

ineffectual grace of semi-Pelagianism and Arminianism. In his "Introduction" to his treatment of common grace, Kuyper thought to guard against this confusion by insisting that "general grace [that is, the common grace that Kuyper is proclaiming in the book] carries no saving seed within itself and is therefore of an *entirely different nature* from particular [that is, saving] grace."[2] He took note of the erroneous assumption that might easily slip in, that Kuyper's doctrine of a common grace of God was an attempt by Kuyper and his allies "thereby...again to dislodge the established foundation of *particular* grace. The notion of 'general' [that is, common] grace...is so easily misused, as if by it were meant *saving* grace, and that is absolutely *not* the case."[3]

With a zeal for this truth that shames most of the contemporary, would-be disciples of the Kuyper of common grace, who have long since embraced and now fiercely defend the universality of saving grace (the well-meant offer), Kuyper affirmed the particularity of the saving grace of God—at the outset of his defense of common grace.

> [Saving] *grace is particular*...Our struggle [on behalf of the particularity of saving grace] has achieved its goal. The particularity of grace, this bastion of our defense, at one time so threatened, is safe once again. In recapturing *the particular character of grace*, we recaptured the heart of our Reformed confession.[4]

---

2   Kuyper, *Common Grace: Noah–Adam*, 12; emphasis is Kuyper's.

3   Ibid., 11; emphasis is Kuyper's.

4   Ibid., 7; emphasis is Kuyper's. Kuyper is referring especially to his recently published defense of particular grace, *Dat de Genade Particulier is* (That grace [*genade*] is particular). This book, which in Kuyper's thinking "recaptured the heart of our Reformed confession," has been translated into English by Marvin Kamps and published under the title *Particular Grace: A Defense of God's Sovereignty in Salvation* (Grandville, MI: Reformed Free Publishing Association, 2001). The relatively cool reception of the translation of Kuyper's work on particular, saving grace by the Reformed, Presbyterian, and Calvinistic community in comparison with the warmth of its reception of the translation of Kuyper's work on common grace indicates that, whereas Kuyper's book on particular grace, in Kuyper's words, recaptured the heart of the Reformed confession, it has not recaptured the heart of the Reformed community of churches and theologians.

As part of his futile endeavor to differentiate two graces of God, Kuyper even gave common grace a different name in his Dutch language from particular, saving grace. Common grace he called "*gratie*"; particular, saving grace he called "*genade*."[5] The English language might try to make this distinction by speaking of "favor" and of "grace." The latter is for the elect alone and sovereignly accomplishes their salvation; the former is for all humans without exception and enables them to produce good culture and thus Christianize the world.

Common grace ("*gratie*," or in English, "favor") is common because God shows it to and actually gives, or bestows, it to and on and in all humans without exception. The very worst reprobate, unbelieving, idolatrous, depraved sinner enjoys common grace, as well as the outwardly moral unbeliever and the elect, believing child of God. Common grace does not save anyone. Salvation is reserved for the particular grace that God has for the elect. But common grace is a genuine love of God for all humans and a real power of divine blessing within and upon all humans.

If this common grace does not save sinners, what does it do to sinners, even the worst of them, we ask. Since it is a grace of God, it must accomplish, and be intended by God to accomplish, something worthwhile, something impressive, something glorifying of God.

The answer is that common grace produces the cultural achievements of the human race—Shakespeare's plays, Beethoven's symphonies, Housman's poetry, Patrick O'Brian's novels, and the philosophies of the pagans Confucius and Plato. Basic to these cultural accomplishments is a certain order and decency in society—the society of a nation and ultimately the society of the whole world of humanity. This order in society with the impressive cultural productions that the order allows for and brings forth is the work of God's common grace. According to Kuyper, "The 'common grace'

---

5   Ibid., 11–12.

of God...produced in ancient Greece and Rome the treasures of philosophic light, and disclosed to us treasures of art and justice...[it] kindled the love for classical studies."[6]

Richard J. Mouw is correct when, in his introduction to the first volume of the translation of Kuyper's *Common Grace*, he describes the power and purpose of common grace as "bringing the cultural designs of God to completion."[7] But, significantly, neither can Mouw avoid linking Kuyperian common grace closely to God's particular, saving grace. In the very next sentence, Mouw attributes to common grace the purpose and power "to prepare the creation for the full coming of the kingdom."[8] Surely the full coming of the kingdom of God in Jesus Christ is the accomplishment of God's saving grace in the cross and resurrection of Jesus Christ, because the fully come kingdom of God is the realm of salvation. Despite the protestations of Kuyper and his contemporary disciples that common grace is to be distinguished from particular, saving grace, neither Kuyper nor his disciples are able to maintain the distinction.

Even for Kuyper himself, as I indicated briefly earlier, cultural products and prodigies are by no means all that Kuyper had in view with his theory of common grace. Kuyper himself distinguished two aspects of common grace: an "external" aspect and an "internal" aspect. The external aspect is such an operation of God in grace as gave the founding fathers of the United States the gift of governing well and therefore gave social order and political good government to the nation. It is such an operation of grace as gave musical ability to the ungodly Mozart and therefore gave the pleasure of beautiful music to us.

---

6   Abraham Kuyper, *Calvinism: Six Stone Foundation Lectures* (Grand Rapids, MI: Eerdmans, 1943), 125.

7   Richard J. Mouw, introduction to Kuyper, *Common Grace: Noah-Adam*, xxv.

8   Ibid.

The Internal Component: "Point of Contact"

Common grace has also an internal component. This aspect of Kuyper's common grace consists of a gracious work of God within unbelieving, ungodly sinners that does several astounding things. It restrains sin in them, so that they are not totally depraved, as otherwise they would be. It preserves in all men, even the most depraved among them, some remnants of the image of God in which the race was originally created, according to Genesis 1 and 2. Some goodness, some genuine goodness, therefore is still to be found in all humans.

> "Common grace" operates in the entirety of our human life, but not in an identical way in every part of this life. There is a common grace directed to the *internal* part of our life and another part of common grace is directed to the *external* dimension of our human life. The former operates everywhere that civic righteousness, family loyalty, natural love, human virtue, the development of public conscience, integrity, fidelity among people, and an inclination toward *piety* permeates life.[9]

Because my controversy in this book is not with Kuyper's lapse from distinctive, biblical, Reformed orthodoxy concerning the gospel of salvation from sin, I merely note here that Kuyper himself was guilty of fundamental departure from the Reformed faith confessed by the Canons of Dordt. Thus Kuyper himself, despite his protestations and warnings to the contrary, opened the way for his disciples, particularly the Christian Reformed Church in its common grace decisions of 1924, to develop his doctrine of common grace into a theology of universal, ineffectual saving grace: the

---

9   Kuyper, *Common Grace: Abraham–Parousia,* 536; emphasis added.

well-meant offer.[10] By his doctrine of common grace, Kuyper denied total depravity. Denial of total depravity leaves the sinner with some spiritual ability to respond positively to the call of the gospel, which call can now be described as an offer of salvation, indeed an offer that is on God's part well-meant, that is, made to all sinners by God with a sincere desire to save them all.

In connection with his affirmation of remains in all sinners of the original image of God, Kuyper states that this remnant of goodness, by virtue of common grace, is the "point of contact" for the gospel and saving grace.

> When Jesus said before his ascension, "Go therefore and make disciples of *all nations...*" [Matt. 28:19], this ordinance of the kingdom was based on the assumption that among all nations there still was a measure of common grace at work. In a nation that had been entirely devoid of common grace or had fallen away, any point of contact [Dutch: *aanrakingspunt*] for the gospel would be lacking, and any mission among such a nation would be unthinkable.[11]

Common grace is a *point of contact* for the gospel!

Contrary to the confession of the Reformed faith that as totally depraved the sinner provides no point of contact for the gospel, common grace now provides such a point of contact. Kuyper's theory of common grace provides an opening to the gospel in the unregenerated, unbelieving sinner. With specific regard to God's coming to Adam after the fall in order to proclaim the gospel of salvation in the seed of the woman (Gen. 3:15), Kuyper writes, "The searching of gracious love is possible only vis-à-vis the creature who, however much that

---

10 For a thorough critique of the well-meant offer, specifically as officially adopted by the Christian Reformed Church, and the demonstration of its inevitable rising out of the theory of Kuyperian common grace, see Engelsma, *Hyper-Calvinism and the Call of the Gospel*. The book also describes the further development of the doctrine of the well-meant offer into universal atonement and the rejection of predestination in the history of the Christian Reformed Church.

11 Kuyper, *Common Grace: Abraham–Parousia*, 529.

creature may be spiritually dead and depraved in his nature, nevertheless still possesses a *point of contact* for divine influence."[12] This point of contact is provided by common grace.

The notion that the sinner himself provides a point of contact to Jesus for his salvation is utter folly. It is as foolish as it would be to affirm that dead Lazarus in the grave provided a point of contact for Jesus' word that raised him from the dead. In fact, this *is* the affirmation of common grace's being a point of contact for the gospel: the spiritually dead sinner has some receptivity to the gospel. But the denial of total depravity and the affirmation of a point of contact for the gospel are worse than folly. They are the corruption of the gospel of salvation by sovereign grace alone, regardless of Kuyper's denial that the theory of common grace trespasses on the precincts of salvation by particular grace.

The fact is that the sole mention of common grace in the Reformed confessions, the three forms of unity, attributes the doctrine to the *Arminians*. The significance of common grace in Arminian theology is exactly that common grace is the point of contact that the sinner provides to God for the entrance and working of saving grace:

> The Synod rejects the errors of those...who teach that the corrupt and natural man can so well use the common grace...or the gifts still left him after the fall, that he can gradually gain by their good use a greater, namely, the evangelical or saving grace and salvation itself. And that in this way God on His part shows Himself ready to reveal Christ unto all men, since He applies to all sufficiently and efficiently the means necessary to conversion.[13]

---

12 Kuyper, *Common Grace: Temptation–Babel*, 312; emphasis added.

13 Canons of Dordt 3–4, error 5, in *Confessions and Church Order*, 171. Explicitly rejected by the Canons here is a doctrine of a common grace of God; the teaching that such a common grace affords access to saving grace; and the idea that there is in God a sincere desire for the salvation of all humans without exception. In inexcusable violation of this their own creed, many, if not most, Reformed churches in North America boldly teach and vigorously defend all the errors condemned by the creed in this article. They do this by their defense of a well-meant offer of the gospel to all hearers as the implication of a common grace of God.

In light of Kuyper's denial of total depravity, it is not surprising that Roman Catholic thinkers, specifically the Roman Catholic theologians of the Acton Institute, can cooperate with the Kuyper of common grace. Rome too teaches that the fall left humans with much goodness—goodness upon which the grace of salvation depends, as well as a goodness that can re-create a good culture.

By virtue of this internal aspect, according to Kuyper, common grace enables all humans to do good, not in the realm of salvation but in the sphere of civil life in society and with regard to everyday earthly life—good in family life, good at work and play, good in the life of the nation. Even though this good is not the supreme good that regeneration produces, it is, nevertheless, *real* good. It is good produced by a grace of God in sinners. It is good in the judgment of God himself. It is good that accomplishes a grand purpose of God with history.

Common grace and its accomplishments in history are of the greatest importance in the thinking of Kuyper and his contemporary disciples. The opening words of Kuyper's treatment of common grace in his large work on the subject are these: "The Reformed paradigm has suffered no damage greater than its deficient development of the doctrine of common grace."[14]

Worldview

Common grace is nothing less than a worldview for the Reformed churches and their members. Common grace explains the world, its history, and God's purpose with the world and history. In light of common grace, we are to view and explain the whole world, the history of the world, and our life in the world. Common grace is a worldview, according to the wisdom and purpose of God himself, the creator and governor of the world and its history.

The very first chapter of the printed form of Kuyper's

---

14 Kuyper, *Common Grace: Noah–Adam*, 3.

lectures on Calvinism at Princeton Theological Seminary in 1898 is titled, "Calvinism a Life-System."[15] "Life-system" is the equivalent for Kuyper of "world-and-life view." In these lectures, in Kuyper's own words, he was describing and prescribing "Calvinism [as a]...*life-* and *world-view.*"[16] Calvinism is, and can only be, such a world-and-life view by virtue of common grace. The message both of the lectures on Calvinism and of the (original) three volumes titled *Common Grace* is that a common grace of God makes Calvinism a worldview, indeed the *biblical* worldview. So much is this the case that, according to Kuyper, as also according to his disciples today, without the doctrine of common grace the Reformed faith and life are ignoble "Anabaptism," that is, shameful, cowardly "world flight."

What common grace Calvinism as a worldview meant for Kuyper, and what it means for his common grace disciples today, Kuyper himself explained. Common grace accomplishes the "untrammeled development of our life [the life of reprobate unbeliever as well as of elect believer] in which to glorify [God] Himself as Creator."[17] Whereas particular, saving grace accomplishes the salvation of sinners and produces the worship of God by the church, common grace achieves good science; art; political government; agriculture, industry, commerce, and navigation; home life and family ties; and high moral standards in the world outside the church.[18] According to Kuyper, "*common grace...* is all encompassing, governing all of history, decisive for our situation, and extending into the farthest future...Our perspective of life and of the entire situation of the world must be formed on the basis of common grace."[19] Peter S. Heslam is correct therefore in analyzing not only Kuyper's

---

15 Kuyper, *Lectures on Calvinism*, 9.

16 Ibid., 171.

17 Ibid., 30.

18 Ibid., 171.

19 Kuyper, *Common Grace: Noah–Adam*, 116–17.

lectures on Calvinism, but also Kuyper's entire common grace project as "creating a Christian worldview."[20]

To ignore or deny a common grace of God, therefore, is deadly serious error for a Reformed Christian and for a Reformed church if common grace and God's purpose with it are indeed a reality. The Reformed community of churches and theologians are well aware of this. With Kuyper, they brand all those who deny common grace as Anabaptists. They read all who deny common grace out of the sphere of legitimate, respectable Reformed Christianity. They are, however, unable to read these churches and theologians out of the realm of *creedal* Reformed Christianity, which ought to give them pause.

What the Reformed community of churches and theologians refuse to consider is that, by the same token, if the theory of common grace is *erroneous*, adoption and practice of the theory are grievous false doctrine with corresponding destructive consequences for those churches that preach it. Nothing less than this is the charge of the Protestant Reformed Churches against the churches and theologians who embrace, promote, and practice the theory of common grace, particularly those who today are making common cause with Rome in Christianizing the world by a common grace of God.

In the controversy over common grace, the stakes are high. The issue is of fundamental importance.

Regardless of whether the theory of common grace is true or false, regarding common grace as a worldview raised a serious problem for Kuyper, as it does also for his disciples today, particularly those now involved in Christianizing the world with the ominous help of Rome. The problem is that God's particular, saving grace in Jesus Christ is also a worldview or the foundation of a worldview. This is the worldview of the gathering and saving of a church out of the nations and the service of God in history by this church.

---

20 Peter S. Heslam, *Creating a Christian Worldview: Abraham Kuyper's Lectures on Calvinism* (Grand Rapids, MI: Eerdmans, 1998). The title of Heslam's book on Kuyper's mission correctly expresses Kuyper's purpose.

Breaching the Antithesis

This gathering of the church includes the antithesis, that is, the separation, antipathy, and warfare between the elect church of believers and their children and the reprobate ungodly. That this separation and enmity are spiritual does not weaken the antithesis but heightens it to the most extreme level. "Come out from among them, and be ye separate" is the efficacious call of God to his believing, holy children in AD 2016 as it was in AD 55 (2 Cor. 6:17). "Know ye not that the friendship of the world is enmity with God?" is a rhetorical question to the common grace disciples of Kuyper today, as it was to members of the apostolic churches in James's time (James 4:4). How do those yoked today with unbelieving Rome and with the world of the ungodly in the grand project of making the world Christian escape the admonition, "Be ye not unequally yoked together with unbelievers" (2 Cor. 6:14)?

This spiritual antithesis and all-out warfare between the world of ungodly men and women, on the one side of the great divide, and the church of elect believers and their children, on the other side of the divide, were established and commanded by God himself at the very dawn of human history and as an essential element of the gospel of grace in Jesus Christ. "I will put enmity between thee and the woman," God said to Satan in the hearing of Adam and Eve, "and between thy seed [reprobate, ungodly, unbelieving humans] and her seed [Jesus Christ and believers and their children]; it shall bruise thy head, and thou shalt bruise his heel" (Gen. 3:15).

That Kuyper and his theological disciples can find in this relation of enmity a friendship of shared grace that enables and demands cooperation of the seed of the devil and the seed of the woman in the grand task of Christianizing the world is a piece of astounding exegesis, at the very least. In fact, it is daring contradiction of and blatant disobedience to the will of God. It is the breaching of the antithesis. Because the antithesis is part and parcel of the gospel of grace itself—Genesis 3:15 is the first revelation and promise of the

Messiah, Jesus!—the venture of Kuyper and his common grace followers is corruption of the gospel.

In view of the prominence of Satan (the one whom God addresses) and of Jesus Christ (the seed of the woman) in the original proclamation of the gospel in Genesis 3:15, what Kuyper and his common grace disciples actually teach in the theory of common grace is that there is friendship between Satan and Jesus Christ and that this friendship allows, indeed requires, them—Jesus the Christ and Satan—to cooperate in the grand work of Christianizing the world.

The silence concerning the antithesis on the part of Reformed churches that embrace Kuyper's theory of common grace and the breakdown of the antithesis in the everyday lives of the members of the Reformed churches who are committed to Kuyper's theory of common grace are apparent to even the most superficial observation in 2016. One striking instance of this breakdown, as of the silence from the pulpit that promotes the breakdown, is the failure of many Reformed parents to maintain and use good Christian schools. Instead, whereas in the past the vast majority of parents provided Christian education to their children, today a high percentage of Reformed parents are content to send their children to the state schools. Often their justification, or excuse, for sending their children to the state schools, where the teaching is godless, the majority of students are unregenerated unbelievers, and the example of life is unholy, is that in the realm of education the children of believers and the children of unbelievers have all things in common. Whether or not explicit appeal to common grace is made, the explanation of this abandonment of distinctive, Christian education is the theology of common grace.

Reformed theologian David Van Drunen contends that use of the state schools is a perfectly legitimate option for Reformed parents. Van Drunen is impressed by the abilities God has given unbelievers to educate the children of the covenant.

Non-Christians often have made greater contributions to human learning than Christians have...We should wish to learn from unbelievers whom God has enabled to understand wonderful things about his creation...We impoverish our children educationally if we unduly cut them off from the accomplishments and contributions of unbelievers...There are still many excellent teachers and fine learning opportunities in public schools.[21]

He avoids grounding his conception of the goodness of the godless education in the state schools in an explicit recognition of common grace. Yet common grace is unmistakably the reason for Van Drunen's recommendation of the public schools, with its implicit rejection of the necessity of Christian education. In support of his recommendation of the Christian's use of the state schools, Van Drunen significantly appeals to the covenant with Noah as the common covenant of a "*common kingdom*."[22] Ignoring the testimony of Romans 1:18–32 concerning what the ungodly invariably do with "natural revelation," namely, hold it under in unrighteousness, Van Drunen bases his advocacy of the education of the state schools on "natural revelation": "natural revelation...comes to all human beings equally under the Noahic covenant."[23]

Clearly implied is that the covenant with Noah was, as Kuyper taught, a covenant of common grace and that this covenant with all humans warrants, if it does not encourage, believers sending their children to the state schools, bypassing the Christian schools. Certainly, Van Drunen does not argue that the public schools are options because they educate as a kingdom and covenant of common total depravity. Nor would he contend that the state schools educate as an institution of the kingdom and covenant of special grace in Jesus Christ. For Van Drunen, therefore, the state schools are

---

21 David Van Drunen, *Living in God's Two Kingdoms: A Biblical Vision for Christianity and Culture* (Wheaton, IL: Crossway, 2010), 184, 186.

22 Ibid., 179; emphasis is Van Drunen's.

23 Ibid., 180.

agencies of common grace, manifestations of the covenant of common grace, and embodiments of the kingdom of common grace. As such, they are good. They render Christian schools unnecessary.

Common grace controls the education of the baptized children of believers. Common grace is the death of good Christian schools. Common grace is the nullifying of the antithesis in the vital matter of the rearing of the covenant children of believing parents "in the nurture and admonition of the Lord" (Eph. 6:4). Common grace commits the lambs of Jesus Christ to the tender mercies of the wolves of the "mystery of iniquity" that is already present and at work in the world (2 Thess. 2:7).

David Van Drunen is a good disciple of his master, Abraham Kuyper. Good disciples always develop the principles of their master further than did, or would, the master himself.

That David Van Drunen has departed radically from the Reformed tradition in the vital matter of the education of covenant children and that therefore Van Drunen's and Kuyper's theory of common grace, nullifying the antithesis, is an innovation in the Reformed churches are evident from the original article 21 of the Church Order of Dordt.

> Everywhere Consistories shall see to it, that there are good schoolmasters who shall not only instruct the children in reading, writing, languages and the liberal arts, but likewise in godliness and in the Catechism.[24]

---

24 Idzerd Van Dellen and Martin Monsma, *The Church Order Commentary* (Grand Rapids, MI: Zondervan, 1941), 93. So deeply embedded in the Reformed tradition and thinking is this concern for the antithetical rearing of the children of the covenant that this article of the Reformed church order was already adopted by a Reformed synod in 1586, barely seventy years after the beginning of the Reformation and some thirty years before the Synod of Dordt. Obviously that early Reformed synod did not countenance a theory of common grace. The contemporary form of this article reads: "The Consistories shall see to it that there are good Christian Schools in which the parents have their children instructed according to the demands of the covenant" (Ibid., 92). Apart from the deeper issue of common grace's breaching the antithesis, Van Drunen's dismissal of Christian education is blatant violation of the Reformed Church Order of Dordt. The theory of common grace does not hold the Reformed traditions (see 2 Thess. 2:15).

The irony of Van Drunen's application of the theory of common grace to the education of covenant children in the public schools is that the master himself warned vehemently against this application of his theory. In a moving chapter in his book of meditations on Christian home life, Kuyper warned against sending covenant children to the (non-Christian) state schools and urged the use of Christian schools. The title of the chapter conveys the message: "Sheep in the Midst of Wolves." Kuyper acknowledged that when they grow up the children of believers "must go out into the world." He added: "But not until he is prepared, until he is matured, until he is well armed and equipped."

Kuyper analyzed the ungodly world of the public schools as wolves. Against them, the child of believers "stands *defenseless*." The spiritual wolves of the public schools "are fanatical in their zeal for the world, and are bent upon inspiring your child...with the spirit of the world. They cannot rest, until your child is become part of the world. They want to make your child like unto themselves...and thus spiritually *devour* him." Concluded Kuyper, here the Kuyper of the antithesis, here the Kuyper who speaks to the Reformed heart and mind, here the Kuyper whom God has used for the welfare of the Protestant Reformed Churches, "First keep your children with Jesus and under the shadow of His wings educate them until they are ready."[25]

Two (Antagonistic) Worldviews

Even though he warned against the application of the theory of common grace that joins believers with unbelievers in the education of their children, Kuyper is himself responsible for this natural development of his theory of common grace. According to Kuyper, we Reformed people have *two different*, really unrelated worldviews, even as God has two different and really unrelated purposes with history. One worldview

---

25 Abraham Kuyper, "Sheep in the Midst of Wolves," in *When Thou Sittest in Thine House*, trans. John Hendrik De Vries (Grand Rapids, MI: Eerdmans, 1929), 171–76.

is the salvation of the church, by particular grace. The other worldview is the Christianizing of culture by common grace.

These two works of God in history run side by side, parallel to each other from creation to the end of the world. Kuyper speaks of a "dual development" of God's work in history.

> On the one hand, common human development of our race was borne only by common grace, resulting in the history of the nations, first in Babylonia, then in Egypt, later in Greece and Rome. In many respects this was a glamorous development that led successively to the sparkling use of the talents God had placed within our race, to the enriching of human life, to the refining of human consciousness, and to the elevation of human self-understanding. It led as well to the application in amazing ways of the human power given us by God, for great inventions, founding kingdoms, producing art, scientific reflection, refining form, and so much more...In this way...immense development can continue for century after century.[26]

"Together with this [development by common grace] an entirely different development occurs in Israel" and in the church of the New Testament by the "particular grace" of God.[27] This work of God accomplishes the salvation of the church by Jesus Christ. Kuyper's "dual development" is, in fact, two different works of God in history, amounting to two different worldviews.

Kuyper insisted that "there is beside the great work of God in *special* grace also that totally other work of God in the realm of *common* grace. That work encompasses the whole life of the world" of all nations. By this work of common grace, God realizes the powers and potentialities of creation in the development of culture in the nations of the world. About this work of God by common grace, Kuyper acknowledges that we "cannot connect [it] with the Kingdom or the content

---

26 Kuyper, *Common Grace: Abraham–Parousia*, 611–12.

27 Ibid., 612.

of our faith." In bold contradiction of the repeated message of the gospel that all things are ours, who are the members of the church (1 Cor. 3:21–23), and that all things work together for the good of the elect (Rom. 8:28–30), Kuyper contends that "the ages must continue not solely for the sake of the elect." Rather, the ages continue "in the interest of developing the world itself to its consummation." That by the development of the world Kuyper had in mind the cultural development of the world, mainly of the ungodly nations and peoples, is evident when he goes on to scorn "every view that would confine God's work to the small sector we might label 'church life.'"[28]

Kuyper's glowing praise of the divine work of common grace raises doubt as to which of the two works of God is more important. The common grace work of God, outside of Jesus Christ, is the more important work in Kuyper's thinking, as is invariably the case with Kuyper's common grace disciples. This is intimated by Kuyper when he states that even in Israel particular grace did not replace common grace but "came alongside common grace." In fact, "common grace is the *foundation* upon which the building of particular grace is erected."[29]

Such is the importance of common grace for all of life, specifically for all of the life of Reformed Christians, that Reformed Christians must regard common grace as

all encompassing, governing all of history, decisive for our situation, and extending into the farthest future. This common grace must be gratefully accepted. Our confession must take account of common grace, and our perspective of life and of the entire situation of the world must be formed on the basis of common grace.[30]

---

28 Kuyper, "Common Grace," in Bratt, *Abraham Kuyper: A Centennial Reader*, 176.

29 Kuyper, *Common Grace: Abraham–Parousia*, 612; emphasis added. Kuyperian James D. Bratt acknowledges that Kuyper "was ambivalent on the point" whether special grace was of "higher rank or worth" than common grace ("Common Grace," in *Abraham Kuyper: A Centennial Reader*, 166).

30 Kuyper, *Common Grace: Noah–Adam*, 116.

The warning follows:

Whoever ignores or underestimates this powerful act of God's grace, and thereby also his *common grace*, distorts his view on life, ends up with a false dualism, and easily runs the risk of allowing his Christian religion to deviate from the *Reformed* track, that is, from the correct track.[31]

How highly Kuyper's disciples esteem the theory of common grace came out in the controversy in the Christian Reformed Church in the early 1920s culminating in the adoption of the doctrine of common grace in 1924. One of the leading proponents of the theory of common grace publicly promoted the theory as "the fountainhead of Reformed thought."[32] This enthusiast for common grace was accurately conveying Kuyper's thought regarding the primacy of common grace in relation to special grace. Kuyper did not shrink from asserting that "the great work of God's grace in Christ presupposes in everything the fruit of common grace."[33] Taking to heart Kuyper's extolling of the fundamental importance of common grace for the whole of the Christian gospel, the Christian Reformed denomination exercised Christian discipline upon a number of officebearers for their rejection of the Kuyperian doctrine of common grace. For the Christian Reformed Church, denial of common grace renders one worthy of exclusion from the kingdom of God.

But the proposal of two worldviews is, by virtue of the proposal itself, the negation of the concept of worldview. Worldview, by definition, is one and only one. Worldview is

---

31 Ibid., 117.

32 H. J. Van Andel, quoted in James D. Bratt, *Dutch Calvinism in Modern America: A History of a Conservative Subculture* (Grand Rapids, MI: Eerdmans, 1984), 110.

33 Abraham Kuyper, *"Invloeden der Gemeene Gratie op de Particuliere Genade"* [Influences of common grace upon particular grace], in *De Gemeene Gratie, Tweede Deel: Het Leerstellig Gedeelte* [Common grace, 2nd part (vol. 2): The doctrinal section] (Amsterdam: Hoveker & Wormser, 1903), 680. Translation of the Dutch is mine. Lest anyone underestimate the fundamental importance of common grace, Kuyper declared that "without common grace [the incarnation of Jesus] would *not* have been the case" (ibid., 679).

one overarching perspective on everything that makes up the world and on everything that takes place in history. Biblical, Christian worldview illumines the whole of God's creation and all of God's work in history as one, and only one, grand work of God, governed by one, and only one, purpose. Not only is the oneness of worldview demanded by the concept itself, but also in the instance of the biblical worldview—the only right worldview—the oneness of worldview is required by the oneness of God the creator and governor. God is not at two purposes with his world, much less at cross purposes with himself in the matter of the history of mankind in his creation.

One last feature of common grace must be mentioned. This important feature is the reason Herman Hoeksema and the Protestant Reformed Churches, and also opponents in Kuyper's own day, rejected the theory of common grace. This feature is that common grace is the ground of the calling of Christians to *cooperate* with the ungodly in the grand work of Christianizing the world. Christians and non-Christians are supposed to share the grace of God—this is the commonness of the *common* grace of God—in order to work together to realize one of God's two great purposes with history: making their society, their nation, and all the world Christian. Reformed Christians share this grace with Roman Catholics and therefore may, can, and must cooperate with them. Reformed Christians share this grace with the ungodly and therefore may, can, and must cooperate with them.

Kuyper sees the sharing of the New Testament church in common grace with the ungodly prefigured in Old Testament Israel. Israel not only possessed common grace, but also outshone the heathens with respect to the exercise of this power.

> Israel...lacked so little in common grace that Israel alone among all nations rather experienced for many centuries the *highest* functioning of common grace, namely, in the *moral-religious* area.[34]

---

34 Kuyper, *Common Grace: Abraham–Parousia*, 525; emphasis is Kuyper's.

Such was the importance of common grace for God's people under the old covenant that for Israel "common grace is the foundation upon which the building of particular grace is erected." "Particular grace [merely] came alongside common grace."[35]

It is significant not only that Kuyper finds common grace also in Israel, God's covenant people, but also that to it he attributes Israel's sense of righteousness and unrighteousness ("moral") and her worship of the one, true God ("religious"). Once again common grace intrudes into the sphere of salvation, despite Kuyper's assurances that his common grace is sharply distinguished and fenced off from "special," saving grace.

Two aspects of this feature of the Kuyperian theory of common grace must strike even the most ardent defender of common grace as at least questionable, if not dangerous. One is the obvious fact that common grace brings the Reformed believer into intimate fellowship and close cooperation with the ungodly unbeliever in a work of realizing one of the two great purposes of God with creation and history. Thus is jeopardized, at the very least, the spiritual separation that God himself has put between believers and unbelievers. "Be ye not unequally yoked together with unbelievers...what part hath he that believeth with an infidel?...come out from among them, and be ye separate, saith the Lord" (2 Cor. 6:14–18). This separation Reformed churches call the antithesis. Already in Kuyper's own time, his "conservative critics... saw in common grace a license for world conformity."[36]

There is another dubious aspect of this feature of the theory of common grace that has the Christian cooperating with the ungodly in Christianizing the world. The Christian is now living all his earthly life in the world not by the power of the particular, saving grace of God in Jesus Christ by the Spirit of Jesus Christ, but by the power of a common grace

---

35 Ibid., 612.

36 James D. Bratt, ed., "Common Grace," in Bratt, *Abraham Kuyper: A Centennial Reader*, 166.

of God—a grace essentially different from the grace of the crucified and risen Jesus and a grace apart from his Spirit. The Christian engages in all of earthly life, or tries to engage in all of earthly life, by some power and wisdom other than the power and wisdom of God revealed in Jesus Christ by the Spirit of Christ.

Not only are the ungodly supposed to be living by a common grace of God and thus creating and developing a Christian culture, but also the godly, in order to work together with the ungodly on this noble, grand project, must in all their everyday, earthly life resist the working of special, particular, saving grace in order to allow common grace to take over. Since God is his perfections, the God of special, saving grace must give way to the god of common grace in the bigger part of the life of the Christian.

This doctrine is a novel form of the heresy of resistible grace condemned by the Reformed church at Dordt: now the believer himself resists the saving grace of God in his own earthly life in the interests of the exercise and sway of common grace.

According to Kuyper, in a statement that by itself exposes the entire theology of common grace as grievous false doctrine, if not nonsense, the "life of our [Christians'] body definitely does not belong to the arena of *particular* grace but most certainly to that of *common* grace."[37] For Kuyper "common grace" is the power that in large part is "the God-ordained means for forming our human person here on earth, and for enriching our spirit, and for developing our character." By common grace, therefore, we live our earthly life. In accordance with the prominent, powerful role of common grace in the Christian's life now, "*the fruit of common grace*" will not "perish forever in the grave, but...will again blossom eternally in that supreme, lavish, and completed knowledge that only eternity can provide us."[38]

---

37 Ibid., 575; emphasis is Kuyper's.

38 Ibid., 586–87.

Kuyper here is making two extravagant claims for his common grace. His contemporary disciples echo these claims. First, the earthly life of the Christian, inner (the forming of personality and so on) and outer (engaging in earthly activities), is largely empowered by common grace, the grace he shares with the ungodly.

> Common grace supplies the believer with the material for fulfilling his calling to be culturally formative and to fight the battle of the Lord in the world of culture...Common grace is *the presupposition of the possibility of* Christian cultural activity.[39]

Kuyper's second extravagant claim is that there will be a reward in eternity corresponding to the amount of common grace one received and to one's energy in diligently exercising this common grace. Indeed, the reward will be nothing less than "the fruit of common grace" in eternity. A Christian like Kuyper, whose prodigious cultural labors, performed by the power of common grace, surpassed the cultural efforts of most Christians, will eternally enjoy a surpassing common grace glory.

To the dismay of Herman Hoeksema and of those who were Protestant Reformed Christians in the world, there will never be an end of the glowing display of common grace, at least display of its fruits and rewards. Not only does the Kuyper of common grace make earthly life unacceptable to us, since Kuyper calls on us to live it by the power of common grace, resisting the power of the grace of God in Jesus Christ; he also bedims to us the glory of heaven. Life there will be aglow with the fruits, rewards, and glories of common grace.

---

39 John Bolt, *A Free Church, a Holy Nation: Abraham Kuyper's American Public Theology* (Grand Rapids, MI: Eerdmans, 2001), 222; emphasis is Bolt's. Bolt is quoting S. U. Zuidema from Zuidema's article "Common Grace and Christian Action in Abraham Kuyper" (see 221 in Bolt).

CHAPTER 3

Creedal and Biblical Basis of the Common Grace Worldview

A fundamental question about this theory and worldview of common grace concerns the confessional and biblical basis of the grandiose vision. That Kuyper has spun out an impressive worldview is undeniable. But does it stand on a biblical foundation? Does it express the world-and-life view of scripture as authoritatively identified and described by the Reformed confessions?

Kuyper virtually acknowledged that there is no basis in the Reformed confessions for this common grace worldview, although he saw this as a weakness not of his theory of common grace but of the confessions. The opening line of his massive work on common grace was an admission of the absence of a doctrine of common grace in the Reformed creeds: "The Reformed paradigm has suffered no damage greater than its deficient development of the doctrine of common grace."[1] What the creeds, particularly the Heidelberg Catechism, indeed the Reformed tradition, failed to do, Kuyper proposed to accomplish in his own systematic, thorough development of the doctrine of a common grace of God, namely, treat the doctrine with some "degree of *coherence* and *completeness*."[2]

---

1   Kuyper, *Common Grace: Noah–Adam*, 3.

2   Ibid., 12–13; emphasis is Kuyper's.

In this work, Kuyper would be opening his "own path" with regard to the theory of common grace.[3]

Canons 3–4.4

Kuyper's attempt to suggest a creedal basis where there is none by repeatedly describing common grace as the "glimmerings of natural light," spoken of in Canons 3–4.4, is a failure. The "glimmerings" are "natural light" or "light of nature," not common grace, and the very article of the Canons that recognizes the "glimmerings" explicitly states that unregenerated humans are "incapable of using it ['this light of nature'] aright even in things natural and civil." Indeed, the unbeliever "renders ['this light of nature'] wholly polluted, and holds it [back] in unrighteousness; by doing which he becomes inexcusable before God."[4]

In light of the alleged importance of common grace for God's very purpose with creation and history, for the calling of the Christian, and for the Reformed faith and life (worldview!), this total lack of support in the creeds is significant. Creedal Reformed Christianity knows nothing of a common grace of God or of a Christianizing of society and the nations. Nothing. *Absolutely* nothing!

The only mention of common grace in the Reformed confessions—and there is a mention of it—is the attribution of the doctrine to the heretical Arminians, in order that the confession will be able to condemn the doctrine of common grace as false doctrine.

> The true doctrine having been explained, the Synod [of Dordt] *rejects* the errors of those...who teach that the corrupt and natural man can so well use the common grace (by which they understand the light of nature), or the gifts still left him after the fall, that he can gradually gain by their good use a greater, namely, the evangelical

---

3   Ibid., 13.

4   Canons of Dordt 3–4.4, in Schaff, *Creeds of Christendom*, 3:588.

or saving grace and salvation itself. And that in this way God on His part shows Himself ready to reveal Christ unto all men.[5]

Although they are loath honestly to admit the absence of a theory and worldview of common grace in the creeds, Reformed theologians and churches today virtually admit this absence by exerting themselves to *concoct* a contemporary creedal basis. The Christian Reformed synod of 1924 did this by quoting only the first half of article 4 of the third and fourth heads of doctrine of the Canons, which teaches "glimmerings of natural light" remaining in the ungodly after the fall. Deliberately, the synod failed to quote or pay attention to the second half of the same article. The second half, as quoted above, explicitly denies that humans can use the light of nature rightly "even in things natural and civil." In fact, this article of the Canons concludes, "[fallen] man... renders [this light of nature] wholly polluted, and holds it [back] in unrighteousness; by doing which he becomes inexcusable before God."[6]

Contrast this statement of the Canons concerning "natural light," which is not the same in the creed as common grace, with Kuyper's and the Christian Reformed Church's emphatic declaration that by the light of nature, which in flagrant disregard of the creed's warning they identify with a common grace of God, the ungodly perform and accomplish a certain real good in the judgment of God. Their total depravity has been restrained so that there remains in them some of the good in which Adam was created. Add to the contrast with the Canons the affirmation of Kuyper and the Christian Reformed Church that by their performance of genuine good in the power of God's common grace, the unbelieving world

---

5 Canons of Dordt 3-4.4, error 5, in *Confessions and Church Order*, 171.

6 On this unrighteous, deceitful tactic of the committee serving the Christian Reformed synod of 1924 with advice concerning the adoption of the third point of common grace, namely, that it quoted only the first sentence of Canons 3-4.4, which teaches glimmerings of natural light in the ungodly, see Herman Hoeksema, "Synod's Proof for the Third Point," in *Protestant Reformed Churches in America*, 388-94.

is fulfilling the grand purpose of God with creation and history of developing a good, even Christian culture.

There is no common grace in this article of the Canons, nor so much as a shred of support for the vast and weighty program of common grace!

Although this confession is fiercely opposed or politely ignored by the majority of Reformed theologians and churches in the twenty-first century, creedal Reformed Christianity confesses that fallen men and women—the wicked world—cannot use the light of nature rightly even in things natural and civil. On the contrary, the Reformed faith continues, the world of unbelieving men and women render the light of nature "wholly polluted" and hold it in unrighteousness. Of the greatest importance, although never recognized, is that this concluding phrase of Canons 3–4.4 applies to the culture of the ungodly the devastating judgment of Romans 1:18–32, as the terminology "holds it [back] in unrighteousness" demonstrates.

According to the inspired testimony of Romans 1:18–32, which Canons 3–4.4 applies to the "light of nature" in the ungodly, the world outside the church is the object not of a grace of God but of the "wrath of God" (v. 18). As the object of the wrath of God, the world of unbelieving men and women do not produce a Christian culture in any sense whatever, but rather "hold the truth in unrighteousness" (v. 18) and change the glory of the incorruptible God, whom they know by virtue of their natural light, into an image (v. 23).

The last stage of their determined rejection of and opposition to the glorious God, whom they know by virtue of natural light, is the shameful perversion of homosexuality and lesbianism. "Their women...change the natural use into that which is against nature: and likewise also the men, leaving the natural use of the woman, burned in their lust one toward another; men with men working that which is unseemly" (vv. 26–27). This shameful sexual lust and behavior are the effect of the wrath of God upon a race that refuses to worship him. In wrath, God gives the ungodly up to vile affections (v. 26).

Western society is now in this last stage of its ungodliness and of the outpouring upon it of the wrath of God, as the developments promoting homosexuality make plain to everyone. At this time of abounding lawlessness and of dreadful, divine wrath, Reformed theologians, churches, and schools make common cause with the world of ungodly men and women to work by a common grace of God on behalf of the Christianizing of this depraved, rebellious, perishing world!

Surely both friends and foes of Kuyperian common grace and its avowed power to Christianize society can agree that the present-day, powerful movement of sodomy and lesbianism is broadly and deeply cultural. It radically affects the fundamental societal institution of marriage and the family. It extends its corrupt and corrupting influence to politics, education, the arts, civil justice, and ultimately to the right of citizenship itself in a nation. As is intimated already, those who condemn homosexuality for the shameful depravity it is and ascribe its presence in Western society to the wrath of God will be violently excluded from society.

This culture, the advocates of common grace assure us, can be Christianized by common grace. "Natural light," the proponents of common grace insist, is a power for the accomplishing of the real good of the world outside of Jesus Christ. Common grace is capable of successfully resisting the wrath of God now giving an ungodly society over to the perversion of wholesale homosexuality, as the stage preliminary to the rising of antichrist.

The advocates of common grace are foolish and blind, as well as theologically in error. The common grace project of Christianizing Western culture in the twenty-first century is sheer madness, as well as the breaching of the antithesis.

"Neo-Calvinism"

The Kuyperian theory of common grace with its Christianizing purpose finds as little support in John Calvin as it does in the Reformed creeds. The popular notion that this common grace of God, although absent from the creeds, represents the theology of Calvin is mistaken. Advocates of common grace in the Reformed community make the claim, but falsely.

Already in Kuyper's own time, learned theologians outside the Reformed churches, who therefore could evaluate objectively Kuyper's claim to be developing the theology of Calvin, noted that the claim was false. Ernst Troeltsch regarded the Kuyper of common grace not as a faithful Calvinist but "as the modernizer of Calvinism." He charged that in his theology of common grace, Kuyper "has drifted far away from Calvin—a fact which Kuyper tried in vain to conceal."[7] Even conservative Christian theologians of Kuyper's own day "charged that his [Kuyper's] so-called Neo-Calvinism had hardly anything to do with Calvin anymore."[8]

In his thorough study of Kuyper's lectures on Calvinism, Peter S. Heslam recognizes that both "would-be followers and opponents alike...reproached [Kuyper] for having broken with traditional Calvinism. Not only conservative Protestants, but modernistic theologians such as B. D. Eerdmans and C. B. Hylkema, condemned Kuyper's...'Neo-Calvinism' for giving totally new meanings to traditional Reformed concepts." With reference particularly to Kuyper's theory of common grace with its aim of Christianizing the world, the modernist Eerdmans declared, "His theology is not Reformed."[9]

Kuyper's theology of common grace was not genuine Calvinism but "*neo*-Calvinism." "*Neo*-Calvinism" describes what Kuyper claimed to be a return to the source in Calvin himself and a genuine development of Calvin's own theology as, in reality, Kuyper's reading into Calvin a theory that was not there at all. Kuyper's theology of common grace was, as the prefix *neo* expresses, a new form of Calvinism.

---

7   Quoted in Hendrikus Berkhof, *Two Hundred Years of Theology*, trans. John Vriend (Grand Rapids, MI: Eerdmans, 1989), 109.

8   Ibid.

9   Quoted in Heslam, *Creating a Christian Worldview*, 241.

The new form was departure from Calvin's own theology. Judged by the standards of Calvin's *Institutes* and especially the authoritative Reformed confessions, Kuyper's elaborate and intricate theology of common grace was Kuyperianism, not Calvinism.

Contemporary Reformed scholars, receptive as they may be to the theory of common grace, with scholarly honesty acknowledge the weakness and doubtfulness of the attempt to ground Kuyper's theory of common grace in the theology of Calvin. James D. Bratt, who has done more with the life and work of Kuyper in recent times than any other American Reformed scholar, writes that in his theology of common grace Kuyper was "laying out...a dramatic new line in Reformed theology. This was the doctrine of common grace, the 'seed' of which he located in some words of Calvin but whose 'manifestation' he elaborated much further than any predecessor had ever tried."[10]

Contemporary Creeds

In view of the complete lack of support for their cultural ambitions and dreams in the Reformed confessions, what various Reformed churches today are doing is drawing up new, contemporary creeds that allow for and even promote common grace, the worldview of common grace, and the Christianizing of the world.

An instance of a modern creed expressing the worldview of common grace that is lacking in all the Reformed and Presbyterian creeds of the past is that of the Christian Reformed Church, "Our World Belongs to God."[11] The Christian Reformed synod of 1983 provisionally approved this "testimony" and sent it to the churches. The department of the Christian Reformed synod that sent the testimony to

---

10 James D. Bratt, *Abraham Kuyper: Modern Calvinist, Christian Democrat* (Grand Rapids, MI: Eerdmans, 2013), 192-93.

11 "Our World Belongs to God" (Grand Rapids, MI: Board of Publications of the Christian Reformed Church, 1984).

the churches referred to the testimony as a "confession."[12] Noticeable is that the worldview of common grace predominates over that of particular grace, if the new creed does not exclude particular grace altogether.

The introduction to this contemporary confession identifies it as a church document "addressing the critical issues of our times." These critical issues are not the truth of creation presently being destroyed in Reformed churches, including the Christian Reformed Church, by evolutionary theory; not the truth of the inspiration of holy scripture presently being undermined in Reformed churches, including the Christian Reformed Church, by the denial of the historicity of Genesis 1–11 and of the infallibility of the entire Bible; not the truth of particular redemption, or limited atonement, presently being opposed in Reformed churches, including the Christian Reformed Church, by the bold proclamation of universal atonement; and not the truth of sovereign predestination presently being contradicted in Reformed churches, including the Christian Reformed Church, by the open denial of reprobation.

These critical issues are specified by the contemporary confession as "marriage, family, education, race, nuclear armaments, and the environment." All the special concerns of "Our World Belongs to God" are summed up as "the biblical idea of the coming kingdom."[13] One who is in the least familiar with the tactic of the promoters of common grace and its intended Christianizing of society to describe their project as the coming of the kingdom of God in history and on earth is alerted to the reality of the confession's promoting the worldview of common grace.

No man can confess and practice two worldviews, for either he will hate the one and love the other, or else he will hold to the one and despise the other. Ye cannot confess particular grace and common grace. This rendering of Matthew 6:24

---

12   Ibid., 7: "'Our World Belongs to God' is your [the churches'] confession."

13   Ibid., 9.

is by no means an imposition on the thought of the teaching of Jesus Christ in the passage. On the contrary, it is a sound application of the thought of the text.

The Covenant with Noah

Kuyper supposed that he had biblical basis for the systematic working out of the doctrine of a common grace of God that had been neglected or overlooked by the Reformed creeds. That biblical basis is the covenant with Noah as recorded in Genesis 9. Beyond all dispute, Genesis 9 with its account of the covenant with Noah after the flood was the main, even fundamental, biblical ground for Kuyper's theory of common grace. With this he began his treatment of common grace in volume 1 of his work on the theory. Correctly, the title of volume 1 of the present-day translation of Kuyper's work on common grace is *Common Grace: Noah–Adam*. With theological accuracy and with faithfulness to the content of Kuyper's treatment of his subject, the title reverses the chronological order of Adam and Noah.

The texts quoted as the headings of the first six chapters of this volume concern Noah and Genesis 9. Typical is the heading over chapter 1, "Introduction": "When God's patience waited in the days of Noah (I Peter 3:20A)." After extensive treatment of the covenant with Noah at the beginning of volume 1, Kuyper returned to this scripture again and again.[14]

It is not an exaggeration to say that Kuyper's theory of common grace stands or falls with his understanding of Genesis 9 and the covenant of God with Noah.

Kuyper explained the covenant with Noah in Genesis 9 as strictly a covenant of common grace. It concerns God's favor

---

14 Some instances of Kuyper's repeated appeals to Genesis 9 and the covenant with Noah, but by no means all of them, include the following: *Common Grace: Noah–Adam*, 7–117; *Common Grace: Temptation–Babel*, 337–68; Kuyper, *Gemeene Gratie*, 2:501ff., 675 (here Kuyper explains the relation of the Noahic covenant to the covenant with Abraham; for Kuyper, the latter covenant of special grace depends on the former covenant of common grace); Abraham Kuyper, *Gemeene Gratie: Het Practische Gedeelte* (Amsterdam: Hoveker & Wormser, 1904), 3:106, 427.

to every human as long as history lasts. God realizes this covenant by withholding another earthly catastrophe like the flood. The Noahic covenant enables all humans, including idolatrous pagans, to develop culture that pleases God, by a work of common grace in them. The covenant with Noah blesses all humans with earthly life, earthly necessities, and earthly comforts. Especially does this covenant restrain sin in all humans, so that they retain some goodness from God's creation of man in his own image, despite the fall of Adam and the race in him. This remnant of the good of creation in God's image enables the fallen, sinful human race outside of Christ to create good culture and thus to develop the earthly creation and its powers to the goal that God had ordained for the creation. In the development of culture by common grace is fulfilled one of the two great purposes of God with his creation and its history.

The covenant with Noah after the flood has nothing whatever to do with salvation. It is wholly and only earthly preservation, earthly development, and earthly blessing. It is a strictly cultural, common grace covenant.

Immediately following his introduction to his massive work on common grace, Kuyper began his treatment of the subject, in the very first line, with these words: "The fixed historical starting point for the doctrine of *common grace* lies in *God's establishment of a covenant with Noah, after the flood*."[15] Concerning the nature of the covenant with Noah, Kuyper asserted that "we are *not* dealing here with a covenant of *particular* grace, but a covenant of *common* grace."[16]

> [The] content of the Noahic covenant lies entirely within the sphere of *natural* life, envisions *temporal* and not *eternal* goods, and applies to unbelievers just as much as it does to those who fear God...The content of this covenant is simply and plainly this: *that until the end of the world,*

15 Kuyper, *Common Grace: Noah–Adam*, 15; emphasis is Kuyper's.

16 Ibid., 28; emphasis is Kuyper's.

the surface of our globe will not again be in a position to be disturbed, but will remain as it is now.

Nothing if not forceful about his identification of the covenant with Noah, Kuyper added, "To identify this content [of the covenant with Noah] in a *spiritual* manner and to wish to explain it in a redemptive way is therefore preposterous."[17] The covenant with Noah was "a covenant of an entirely different kind" from the covenant of grace in Jesus Christ.[18] The grace of the covenant with Noah was not saving grace (*genade*) but common grace (*gemeene gratie*).[19]

Kuyper's argument on behalf of this theology of the covenant with Noah includes that the name of God in Genesis 9 is not the covenant name, Jehovah or *Yahweh*, but the name *Elohim*, which reveals his deity or godhead. Kuyper also appealed to the universality of the covenant with Noah as proof that this is a covenant of common, non-saving grace with all humans. The covenant with Noah extends to all nations and peoples: Noah, his three sons, and their descendants (Gen. 9:9).

Yet another ground for Kuyper's view of the covenant with Noah as a covenant of common grace was Kuyper's assumption that Ham was a reprobate. Making plain that he viewed the covenant of saving grace as governed by election, Kuyper contended that since the covenant was with Ham as well as with his two brothers, the covenant with Noah had to have been a covenant of common grace.

Then Kuyper argued for a covenant of common grace on the ground that the covenant with Noah was also with the animal world (Gen. 9:10). Only a covenant of common grace includes animals, according to Kuyper.

Without ignoring Kuyper's appeal to the particular name of God that appears in the account of the covenant with

---

17 Ibid., 33; emphasis is Kuyper's.

18 Ibid., 44.

19 Kuyper, *Common Grace: Temptation–Babel*, 353.

Noah in Genesis 9, one may rightly conclude that the main ground for explaining the covenant with Noah as a covenant of common grace is its universality, with regard to both humans and animals.

CHAPTER 4

Reformed Critique of Kuyper's Common Grace Worldview: The Confessions

I frankly refer to my criticism of this common grace theory, worldview, and project as the Protestant Reformed critique, although I regard it as the soundly *Reformed* critique—the critique made by the Reformed tradition and especially by the Reformed creeds. I know of no other Reformed denomination of churches today that opposes this theory and its worldview. If other Reformed churches do oppose it, they are careful to keep their objection out of the public eye.

In the early 1900s in the Netherlands, the influential Kuyper and his nearly equally influential colleague Herman Bavinck overwhelmed the opposition. And there was opposition. The opposition charged that Kuyper's theory of common grace would make the churches worldly. Reformed men feared that the common grace philosophy of the Christianizing of culture would prove to be ecclesiastical suicide, rather than a reviving of the world.

In the early 1920s, when the theory of the Christianizing of the world by Kuyper's common grace rolled over the Christian Reformed Church like a tidal wave, one young Christian Reformed minister resolutely took a stand against common grace and therefore against the Kuyper of common grace: Herman Hoeksema.

Today, one denomination of Reformed churches says no, loudly and uncompromisingly, to Kuyperian common grace, specifically with regard to its cultural pretensions. One denomination is known throughout the Reformed church world for saying no—not honored for saying no, but known: the Protestant Reformed Churches in America.

I now indicate why we say no to Kuyper's common grace and its crusade of Christianizing the world.

I have already called attention to the total lack of confessional basis for this supposedly fundamental doctrine and supposedly urgent calling of the church and of the Christian. Kuyper himself acknowledged the absence of any recognition of common grace and its grand work of Christianizing the world in the Reformed creeds. This absence of any doctrine of common grace and its worldview in the creeds is no insignificant matter. That Reformed churches and theologians continue to magnify the doctrine, its worldview, and its alleged calling for Reformed churches and members, despite any creedal basis for all of this, is simply building castles in the air.

The Reformed Confessions

But matters are still worse for the doctrine of cultural common grace in light of the Reformed confessions. The confessions condemn the theory. They condemn essential elements of the theory *explicitly*. For one thing, the creeds teach the total depravity of every human by nature, so that the unsaved person can do no good, not even in things natural and civil. The creeds teach total depravity as a *reality*, not merely as a possibility apart from a common grace of God. Question 8 of the Heidelberg Catechism declares that all humans are "so far depraved that we are wholly unapt to any good, and prone to all evil...unless we are born again by the Spirit of God."[1]

By this creedal statement alone, the entire common grace edifice—that grand castle in the air—of Kuyper and his

---

1 Heidelberg Catechism Q&A 8, in Schaff, *Creeds of Christendom*, 3:310.

contemporary epigones crumbles. The depraved spiritual condition of all humans renders us incapable of "any good," including the good of creating a culture that carries out some important purpose of God with creation and history, that pleases God, and that constitutes a basis for the cooperation of the godly with the ungodly. The spiritual condition of all humans is a proneness to "all evil," which includes cultural evil, so that all the natural man does or can do in eating and drinking, in marriage and family, in work and play, in art and politics is sin. Not only in the sphere of worship, but also in the realm of culture the natural man sins and can only sin.

The sole deliverance from this condition of depravity, according to question 8 of the catechism (which was binding on Kuyper as it is on his disciples in Reformed churches today), is that one is "born again by the Spirit of God." Exposed therefore as erroneous, indeed as false doctrine, is the basic teaching of Kuyperian common grace that there is also deliverance from total depravity by a common grace of God, which, of course, does not regenerate anyone.

An even clearer and stronger condemnation of Kuyper's theory of common grace, now bewitching most of Reformed Christendom, is article 4 of the third and fourth heads of doctrine of the Canons of Dordt. Confessing the spiritual corruption of all fallen, unsaved humans, Socrates, Mozart, Shakespeare, and Benjamin Franklin as well as Nero, Rabelais, Ringo Starr, and Feuerbach, this article of the Canons denies that any human, regardless of the brightness of the "light of nature" remaining in him, is capable of doing what is right and good "in things natural and civil." On the contrary, all humans who are not converted by the Spirit of Jesus Christ render even the natural light "wholly polluted."[2]

Fatal—*fatal*—to Kuyper's theory of cultural common grace is the truth that natural light is not grace. By their competent, often brilliant, use of natural light in things "natural and civil," unbelievers do not perform good in the judgment

---

2   Canons of Dordt 3-4.4, in ibid., 3:588.

of God, are not engaged in the commendable labor of Christianizing the culture, and offer no ground for believers to cooperate with them in carrying out one of God's (alleged) great purposes with the creation and with history.

The Reformed doctrine of total depravity, taught by the third and fourth heads of the Canons, describes a reality, not a mere possibility. It exposes men and women as they are, not as they otherwise would be were it not for common grace. It condemns the cultural life and work of unbelievers as well as their worship and service of their gods. It condemns the cultural life and work of unbelievers as sin. And sin does not Christianize. One might as well say that black whitens or that the devil sanctifies.

Today as well, the charge of the Reformed faith against the advocates of common grace and their project of Christianizing society and the world—the contemporary alliance of Reformed theologians and the Acton Institute—is that they deny the biblical and creedally Reformed doctrine of total depravity. This charge is not only a strong one. It is damning.

Kuyper was well aware of the fact that his theory of common grace was a denial of the Reformed, indeed historic, orthodox *Christian*, doctrine of total depravity. Rather than give up his theory, however, he stubbornly defended it by opposing the doctrine of total depravity.

Already Augustine in the early fifth century after Christ had confronted the apparent refutation of his and the Christian church's doctrine of total depravity by the seeming good works of the heathens. Not all were fornicators and adulterers; some were loyal to wife and family. Not all were lawless threats to their society and nation; some were self-sacrificing patriots of their nations and promoters of the earthly good of their societies. Not all were drunken sots; some were marvelous artists and talented writers.

Confronted by appeals to such heathens by the foes of his doctrine of total depravity, Augustine did not compromise the biblical truth that is basic to the gospel of grace. He did not appeal to some remnants of the image of God in fallen mankind. He did not invent a theory of common grace to explain the seemingly noble, virtuous deeds and lives of some ungodly men and women. Rather, Augustine described these deeds as "splendid," or "glittering," "*vices*." The seemingly noble and virtuous deeds of some unbelievers are not genuine good works, belying the total depravity of these heathens. They are vices, and only vices, that is, sins. But they are sins that glitter, whereas other sins, for example, adultery, drunkenness, murder, and rioting, are sordid sins.

Arguing for his theory of common grace by explicitly appealing to the "virtues of the heathen," among which Kuyper counts the writings of the pagan pederast Plato and of the heathen idolater Cicero, Kuyper rejects, indeed scoffs at, Augustine's explanation of the seemingly noble deeds of the ungodly as "splendid vices."

> True, some people save themselves from this awkward position [the apparent contradiction of total depravity by the seemingly noble deeds of unbelievers] by speaking of the virtues of unbelievers as "splendid vices."[3]

Regarding such works as "splendid vices," says Kuyper, "is a subterfuge, which lacks earnestness."[4] Thus Kuyper denied the Reformed, Christian doctrine of total depravity. He denied total depravity by and in the interests of his theory of common grace.

Grace and Providence

Yet another fundamental doctrine of the creeds that exposes and condemns Kuyperian common grace is the creeds' sharp, clear, and emphatic distinguishing of God's *providence* from his grace and blessing. A serious, indeed fundamental, and completely inexcusable error of Kuyper and his disciples is their confusion of providence and grace. For Kuyper, in his promotion of the theory of common grace, physical life,

---

3   Kuyper, *Lectures on Calvinism*, 122.

4   Ibid.

health, food and drink, the ordering of earthly life by police and army, and material prosperity in general are grace and blessing—divine, *common* grace and blessing.

Identification of physical well-being with grace settles the issue whether God is gracious to the ungodly, for the health and wealth of the ungodly are obvious to all. If physical prowess, earthly bounties, and material ease are grace, Esau, the Babylonians, Emperor Nero, and my godless, adulterous, blasphemous, Sabbath-desecrating, but comfortably well-off neighbors were, and are, blessed by God with grace, be it common grace.

In a chapter devoted to proving common grace in the bodily life of the wicked, Kuyper contends that "we can still speak of *prosperity* and *well-being* and *health*...[as] exclusively a fruit of this *common grace* of our God." He adds, "If even for a moment we feel really good and robustly healthy, we owe it to [common grace] alone."[5]

The continued existence of the earthly creation as a habitation for the human race; the earth's bringing forth of bread for man; the spectacular changing of the seasons; the flower on the rose bush—all "shows us common grace." So important is this recognition of common grace in whatever pleases humans and enhances human life in the earthly creation that

> we cannot arrive at a clear world-view, a clear vision of life and of nature, unless we remember at every point that the *original* perished in what at present bears the mark of the *curse*, and unless at the same time we discern the *reining in* of that curse in the work of *common grace* that calls for our adoration of God.[6]

The very existence of the creation after the fall is the work

---

5   Kuyper, *Common Grace: Temptation–Babel*, 327–28; emphasis is Kuyper's.

6   Ibid., 336; emphasis is Kuyper's. The translators have softened Kuyper's paean to the all-glorious common grace here. Kuyper wrote of the "reining in of that curse in the *adorable work of common grace*." The Dutch is *"in het aanbiddelijk werk der gemeene gratie"* (Kuyper, *De Gemeene Gratie*, 1:268). There is nothing in the original of our adoring *God*, as the translation would have it. Kuyper would have us adore *the work of common grace*—not merely acknowledge it but *adore* it.

of God's common grace. By common grace, "the world as such continued to exist...Through common grace alone it was possible for what existed to continue existing, and the manifold wisdom of God came forth in the fruit of its activity as well."[7] Kuyper reaffirmed this confusion of providence with common grace regarding the upholding of the creation: "It is exactly common grace that, over against curse and death, kept the reality of things in existence and still holds [them in existence]."[8]

In keeping with his attributing to common grace the maintenance of creation, Kuyper also credited common grace with the governing of history. So important is common grace that "if no common grace had been functioning, then that piece of history [between Christ's ascension and his return] would have been inconceivable...This broad historical development finds its propellant and motivation only in the existence of common grace."[9] Whether New Testament or Old Testament, "nowhere would a historical development have been thinkable [without common grace]."[10] The entire history of redemption depends upon common grace. "All this [history of redemption] has become possible only through common grace."[11]

All that Kuyper attributes to common grace regarding the continuing existence of the earth; the course of history, whether secular or sacred; and the enjoyment of health and the bounties of the creation by the reprobate ungodly, the Reformed confessions ascribe to the providence of God. By his providence God upholds and governs his creation; by his providence God governs history; by his providence God produces the lovely rose amid the thorns; by his providence God revolves the seasons; by his providence God gives health and wealth to the ungodly, who curse him and are unthankful; by

---

7   Kuyper, *Common Grace: Abraham–Parousia*, 604, 606.

8   Kuyper, *De Gemeene Gratie*, 2:679. The translation of the Dutch is mine.

9   Ibid., 2:544.

10 Ibid., 2:545.

11 Ibid., 2:546.

his providence through police and army God maintains some order in a nation.

Providence, however, is not grace. Providence is divine power. In the definition of the Reformed creed, providence is "the almighty and every where present power of God, whereby, as it were by his hand, he still upholds heaven and earth, with all creatures, and so governs them."[12] Gifts of providence, for example health, earthly riches, a good job, and the order kept by civil government—all the good, earthly things adduced by Kuyper as evidences of a common grace of God—are not inherently, necessarily, and always grace and grace's blessings.

The Reformed confessions sharply distinguish gifts of providence from divine grace and blessing. Treating the fourth petition of the model prayer, "Give us this day our daily bread," the Heidelberg Catechism states that "without thy [God's] blessing neither our care and labor nor thy gifts can profit us."[13] Bread and other earthly necessities and luxuries are gifts from God. But they are not inherently "blessings," that is, gifts that come to a human in God's grace toward him and that accomplish his good. Divine blessing, flowing from the grace of God, is not identical with the gift. Nor does blessing necessarily accompany the gift. Blessing is distinct from the gift itself.

One may receive the gift of bread without any divine blessing, as do all unbelievers, who neither seek their bread from God, acknowledge bread to be God's gift, thank him for bread, nor devote the life sustained by bread to God. If the bread does not come with blessing, it comes with the divine curse, out of God's disfavor or wrath. "The curse of the LORD is in the house of the wicked," including his cupboards, refrigerator, and freezer (Prov. 3:33).

A grievous weakness of the theory of common grace, which identifies good earthly things with the (common)

---

12 Heidelberg Catechism Q&A 27, in Schaff, *Creeds of Christendom*, 3:316.

13 Heidelberg Catechism Q&A 125, in ibid., 3:353.

grace of God, is its implication that a lack of good earthly things or affliction with evil earthly things, for example poverty, sickness, and other miseries, represents God's disfavor and expresses God's curse toward the distressed believer. If health is grace to the ungodly, sickness is wrath to the godly. The theory of common grace explicitly pronounces blessing on the wealthy, healthy godless man or woman. Implicitly, the theory curses the poor, starving, sickly saint. Thus the rich man in Jesus' parable in Luke 16:19–31 was the object of God's grace and blessing while he lived, whereas Lazarus was devoid of the divine blessing, if he was not cursed.

Scripture denies that grace and blessing consist in earthly things and circumstances. The prosperous of Psalm 73:1–12, "the ungodly, who prosper in the world; they increase in riches" (v. 12), are cursed with and by their prosperity, for that prosperity is God's setting them in slippery places, to slide into the destruction and desolation of eternal hell (vv. 18–19). Some grace! Some blessing! On the other hand, the poor, plagued believer of the psalm (vv. 13–14) is blessed in and with his poverty and earthly misery because in this way God guides him so as afterward to receive him to glory (v. 24).[14]

The intensely practical, spiritual purpose of Psalm 73 must not be overlooked. Recognition that the prosperity of the wicked is not divine grace to them but God's curse casting them down to eternal destruction keeps the psalmist, and every child of God, from slipping and falling into sheer unbelief and despair, as though a life of faith and holiness is vain while a life of ungodliness is the object of divine blessing. The psalmist reveals this practical purpose of the psalm in the opening verses: "As for me, my feet were almost gone; my

---

14 For a thorough exposition of Psalm 73, which psalm is devastating to the theory of common grace and decisive regarding the controversy over common grace, see David J. Engelsma, *Prosperous Wicked and Plagued Saints: An Exposition of Psalm 73* (Jenison, MI: Reformed Free Publishing Association, 2007). John Calvin explains Psalm 73 as a warning against our readiness "to imagine, that, since God grants them [the ungodly] so much of the good things of this life, they are the objects of his approbation and favour" (*Commentary on the Book of Psalms* [Grand Rapids, MI: Eerdmans, 1949], 3:126).

steps had well nigh slipped. For I was envious at the foolish, when I saw the prosperity of the wicked" (vv. 2–3).

Kuyper's theory of common grace is the final push upon the child of God whose "steps had well nigh slipped" (v. 2) because of the earthly prosperity of the ungodly. Hearing from Kuyper and his disciples that the earthly prosperity and comforts of the wicked (which by their contrast with his own earthly distress already are the occasion of severe temptation to him) are in fact God's grace toward and blessing of the ungodly, the afflicted believer must lose his spiritual footing altogether, did not the testimony of Psalm 73 hold him up. Losing one's spiritual footing would be unbelief and damnation.

The theory of common grace is no mere, minor theological dispute. On the contrary, it concerns a matter of life-or-death, practical importance for the Christian faith and life.

CHAPTER 5

Reformed Critique of Kuyper's Common Grace Worldview: Scripture (1)

With regard to his fundamental biblical basis for his theory of common grace, Kuyper was in error. That biblical basis was God's covenant with Noah in Genesis 9. Kuyper began his exposition of common grace with the covenant with Noah. To that covenant he returned, again and again, in his development and defense of common grace.

Kuyper, you will recall, explained the covenant with Noah as a covenant of common grace. It was a covenant with all humans, reprobate and elect, believers and unbelievers, saints and ungodly alike. It concerned only earthly life, earthly things, and earthly circumstances. It did not involve spiritual blessing and salvation. Its source was a favor or love of God toward all humans, desiring their temporal welfare and prosperity. The expression of this favor of God in the Noahic covenant was the bestowal upon all humans of material goods—healthy life, rain and sunshine in season, food and drink, riches and ease.

According to Kuyper, although he struggled to posit some connection between the covenant with Noah and the covenant of grace in Jesus Christ, the covenant with Noah was essentially different from the covenant of grace established with Abraham, fulfilled by Jesus Christ, and realized with the elect church. The covenant with Noah was a covenant of *common* grace. That covenant was "a covenant of an entirely different kind" from the covenant of saving grace in Jesus Christ.[1]

> That *content* of the Noahic covenant lies entirely within the sphere of *natural* life, envisions *temporal* and not *eternal* goods, and applies to unbelievers just as much as it does to those who fear God...The content of this covenant is simply and plainly this: *that until the end of the world, the surface of our globe will not again be in a position to be disturbed, but will remain as it is now.*[2]

Railing against the teaching that the covenant with Noah was a manifestation of God's covenant of saving grace in Christ with an intensity that betrays some doubt on Kuyper's part about his own doctrine, Kuyper added that "to identify this content [of the covenant with Noah] in a *spiritual* manner and to wish to explain it in a redemptive way is therefore preposterous."[3]

"Preposterous"? Not merely mistaken but "preposterous"? "Methinks thou dost protest too much"!

Calvin on the Noahic Covenant

Kuyper's interpretation of the covenant with Noah as a covenant of common grace and therefore essentially different from the covenant of saving grace in Jesus Christ is inexcusable simply in view of the fact, which Kuyper himself frankly acknowledged, that all the outstanding Reformed theologians before him explained the covenant with Noah as a manifestation of the covenant of saving grace. Kuyper mentioned Pareus, Perkins, Mastricht, and Rivet—a list of Reformed luminaries. "In particular, Pareus, Perkins, and Mastricht understood it [the covenant with Noah] in this more restricted sense [as the covenant of saving grace 'with

---

1   Kuyper, *Common Grace: Noah–Adam*, 44.

2   Ibid., 33; emphasis is Kuyper's.

3   Ibid.

believers only'], and Rivet also uses an expression that seems to indicate that he was of the same opinion." Kuyper admits that his explanation of the covenant with Noah "does not agree with this analysis."[4]

Kuyper's appeal to John Calvin in support of his explanation of the covenant with Noah as a covenant of common grace, in distinction from the covenant of saving grace, is mistaken. Contrary to Kuyper's claim, Calvin viewed the covenant with Noah as a revelation of the covenant of saving grace in Jesus Christ. In his commentary on Genesis 6–9, the account of the flood and of God's covenant with Noah, Calvin states that "the ark was an image of the Church."[5] For Calvin, "Noah's deliverance from the universal deluge was a figure of baptism." Significantly, Calvin appeals here to 1 Peter 3:21, adding that "the method of the salvation, which we receive through baptism, agrees with this deliverance of Noah."[6]

Regarding the salvation of animals in the ark, of which Kuyper makes much on behalf of a common grace covenant, as though God's covenant of salvation in Jesus Christ does not include animals, Calvin says this: "On account of the salvation promised to man, his [God's] favor is extended to brute cattle, and to wild beasts." Calvin does not deduce from the saving of animals in the ark and the inclusion of animals in the covenant with Noah that the covenant with Noah was different from the covenant of salvation in Jesus Christ, as was the argument of Kuyper. Rather, Calvin finds in the salvation of the animals the same favor that God has toward his own children and additional proof of this favor to them:

> If, on account of the salvation promised to man, his favour is extended to brute cattle, and to wild beasts; what may we suppose will be his favor towards his own children,

---

4   Ibid., 26–27.

5   John Calvin, *Commentaries on the First Book of Moses Called Genesis* (Grand Rapids, MI: Eerdmans, 1948), 1:257.

6   Ibid., 273.

to whom he has so liberally, and so sacredly, pledged his faithfulness?[7]

In his commentary on 2 Peter 3:5, important New Testament light on the history of Noah and the flood, Calvin writes that the significance of the flood was eternal damnation for the wicked, who perished in it, and not merely temporal death as Kuyper argued: "How can the wicked [today] escape the deluge of divine wrath, since the whole world was once destroyed by it?"[8] Implied is that the salvation of Noah and his family was not merely a temporal deliverance from a natural calamity as Kuyper held but, as to its meaning, a spiritual salvation, the salvation that is in Jesus Christ and that is bestowed by the saving grace of God.

Much as he exerted himself to enlist Calvin in support of his conception of the covenant with Noah as a covenant of common grace, Kuyper was compelled to acknowledge that "Calvin and the Calvinists...focused too exclusively on the covenant of *saving* grace, while paying too little attention to the covenant of *common* grace...[as] this covenant of common grace is...clearly delineated in Noah's history."[9]

Although promoting Kuyper's program of Christianizing the world by the allegedly Calvinistic power of a common grace of God, English theologian Peter S. Heslam freely grants that "common grace...was not normally considered one of the essential or fundamental doctrines of Calvinism, and does not occupy a prominent position in Calvin's theology."[10]

Doctrinal Modernism

Here I take up the third element of the "deep background" of this book, to which I alluded in the opening chapter. It is widely recognized today by both their allies and their foes

7   Ibid., 277.

8   John Calvin, *Commentaries on the Catholic Epistles* (Grand Rapids, MI: Eerdmans, 1959), 397.

9   Kuyper, *Common Grace: Temptation–Babel*, 356–57; emphasis is Kuyper's.

10 Heslam, *Creating a Christian Worldview*, 140.

that the entire common grace project of Kuyper and Bavinck, with its avowed purpose of impacting Dutch society and then the entire world, was motivated not by the Dutch theologians' determination to do justice to a basic but neglected aspect of the Reformed faith nor by their discovery of a hitherto overlooked teaching of the Bible, but by the emphasis in their day by modernist theologians on the need to relate the church closely to the world.

For longer than a hundred years, the emphasis of the apostate, modernistic theology of Europe was that the main calling of the Christian church was to relate itself to the world of ungodly thought and conduct in such a way as to cooperate with the world in making the world's culture better, even Christian. The task of the church was to "mediate" between the gospel and the culture. For Kuyper and Bavinck, the way for Reformed theology and theologians to accommodate this prevalent thinking, especially in light of the distinctively Reformed doctrine of particular grace, implying the reality of the antithesis (which does not allow for mediation), was the theory of a common grace of God.

The Kuyperian theory of common grace, with its program of cooperation with the world of the ungodly in order to Christianize the world, therefore is nothing more than Kuyper's caving in to the modernist theological thinking of his day. It represents nothing more than orthodoxy's concession to unbelieving modernism. It is nothing more than a yielding to a perennial threat to the church, that she conform to and ally herself with the world of the ungodly. Mediation between gospel and culture always ends in the compromising of the gospel and its way of life (genuine Christian culture).

This analysis of Kuyper's theory of common grace, with its accompanying program of the Christianizing of the Netherlands, is that of Hendrikus Berkhof, prominent Dutch theologian and by no stretch of the imagination an enemy of Kuyper's cultural thinking and efforts. Berkhof regards Kuyper's theory of common grace as a "neo-confessional alternative" to the liberals' attempt to relate positively the

Christian faith and the culture of the world of the ungodly. Berkhof observes correctly that "conservative Christians charged that his [Kuyper's] so-called Neo-Calvinism [Kuyper's theology of common grace] had hardly anything to do with Calvin anymore." With insight, or honesty, that is rare among Kuyper's ardent disciples, Berkhof concludes: "In theology—*apart from his broad development of the doctrine of common grace*—Kuyper closely followed the Calvinistic tradition, even in its scholastic form."[11]

"Apart from his broad development of the doctrine of common grace"!

Reformed believers who love the theology of John Calvin and reject the theory of common grace need not quail before the reproach that they are un-Calvinistic. Kuyper's elaborate theory of a common grace of God with its Christianizing program is missing from a prominent, if not the main, line of the Reformed tradition, beginning with John Calvin himself.

The more serious aspect of the absence of a doctrine of a covenant of common grace with Noah in the Reformed tradition is the silence on such a covenant in the Reformed creeds. This too Kuyper recognized.

> In the church's faith confessions justice is hardly ever done to this former work of God [the supposed covenant with Noah], and it is remarkable how little attention is paid

---

11 Berkhof, *Two Hundred Years of Theology*, 108–11; emphasis is added. Also Peter S. Heslam observes that Kuyper's development of his theory of common grace "was not unrelated...to the academic theological world of his day." Kuyper was responding to, if not influenced by, the modernist theology of the day, which "placed the church-world relationship firmly back onto the theological agenda." Not scripture and the Reformed confessions but modernist theological thinking framed Kuyper's thinking concerning "the relationship of Christianity to culture" (*Creating a Christian Worldview*, 118). According to Heslam, Kuyper's worldview of common grace "brought Kuyper severe criticism from would-be followers and opponents alike, who reproached him for having broken with traditional Calvinism" (Ibid., 241). Heslam's judgment is that Kuyper's "doctrine of common grace...is not a major element in traditional Calvinistic theology" (Ibid., 259). This is understatement. But it is also implied rebuke to the fanatical proponents of Kuyper's theory and program of common grace for their charge that those who deny common grace have departed from a fundamental tenet of Calvinism.

to the Noahic covenant in the manuals of theological dogmatics.[12]

Kuyper had no support in the main line of the Reformed tradition, much less in the creeds, for his novel interpretation of the Genesis flood and of the covenant with Noah in Genesis 9. It is not to the credit of contemporary Reformed theologians that they have allowed Kuyper to lead them down the primrose path of regarding the covenant with Noah as a covenant of common grace, simply in view of the overwhelming, contrary witness of the Reformed tradition.[13]

More on the Noahic Covenant

It is highly suspicious that Kuyper's explanation of the flood, of the salvation of Noah and his family by the flood, and of the covenant with Noah differs radically from the Reformed tradition, beginning with Calvin. It is fatal to Kuyper's and his common grace disciples' explanation of Noah, the flood, and the covenant with Noah that this explanation is contradicted by the clear, repeated witness of New Testament scripture.

There are several New Testament references to and descriptions and applications of Noah and the flood: Hebrews 11:7, 1 Peter 3:20, and 2 Peter 2:5. Each one explains that history, including the covenant with Noah, in terms of *spiritual* salvation, as well as of the *spiritual* wickedness and eternal damnation of the wicked who perished in the flood.

Second Peter 2:5 is representative. Immediately after the warning of verse 4, of God's condemnation of the rebellious angels, casting them "down to hell," verse 5 adds this warning: "And spared not the old world, but saved Noah the eighth person, a preacher of righteousness, bringing in the

---

12 Kuyper, *Common Grace: Noah–Adam*, 36.

13 Which fault the theologians aggravate by dismissing, out of hand, the contemporary witness that maintains the traditional Reformed explanation of the deliverance of Noah and his sons by the flood as nothing but un-Reformed "Anabaptism."

flood upon the world of the ungodly." The history of Noah and the flood, including the covenant with Noah, does not teach a common grace blessing and earthly preservation of ungodly culture and its ungodly practitioners. Rather, it teaches the *spiritual* salvation of those who are righteous by faith alone (Heb. 11:7), by means of the eternal destruction of their ungodly enemies.

So contrary to Kuyper's theory of the flood, the deliverance in the ark, and the covenant with Noah is the biblical account, especially the interpretation and application of the history of Genesis 6–9 in the New Testament, that one can only conclude that Kuyper was desperate for some biblical basis of his common grace theory.

Regarding Kuyper's argument that the biblical record of the covenant with Noah in Genesis 9 does not use the covenant name of God—the name "Jehovah"—but rather the name that reveals him as the sovereign God over all nations and all the earth—the name "Elohim"—the refutation is that Genesis 8 and Genesis 9 are one closely related unit of scripture. Chapter divisions in the Authorized Version, or any other translation, are not part of the inspired original scripture. Closely related to the establishment of the covenant with Noah in Genesis 9, indeed fundamental to it, is the sacrifice of Noah and the Lord's response to that sacrifice in Genesis 8:20–22. That the end of Genesis 8 is intimately related to the covenant with Noah that is more fully revealed in Genesis 9 is evident from the Lord's promise at the end of Genesis 8 that he will not "smite any more every thing living, as I have done" (v. 21).

Noah's altar and sacrifice in Genesis 8:20 are the basis of the covenant with Noah of Genesis 9. In that sacrifice, the "Lord smelled a sweet savour" (8:21). On the basis of the sacrifice and its sweet savor, the Lord said in his heart that he would lift the curse from the earthly creation and never again smite every living thing as he had just done in the flood (8:21). That altar was, in reality, the cross of Jesus Christ. That sacrifice was the offering up of the Son of God in human flesh as the expiation of the sins of the world. That sweet smell in the divine nostrils was the satisfying of the justice of God.

The name of God used in Genesis 8:20–22 is Jehovah (in the AV "LORD"). This is the covenant name of God—the name that reveals God as the God of the covenant of particular, special, saving grace. The God who blessed Noah and established with him his covenant was Jehovah. On Kuyper's own reckoning, namely, that a covenant established by God in his name Jehovah is the covenant of particular, saving grace, the covenant with Noah was this covenant.

Such is the importance of the covenant with Noah in Kuyper's doctrine of common grace that with the failure of his false theology of the covenant with Noah falls Kuyper's entire theory of common grace.

The Reformed baptism form also speaks to the nature of the covenant with Noah. This form views the flood as God's punishing of the unbelieving world and as the salvation of Noah and his family. Obviously, the baptism form regards the salvation of Noah and his family as spiritual salvation, inasmuch as the deliverance of Noah by the flood was an Old Testament symbol of Christian baptism. The creed's explanation of the salvation of Noah as symbolic of baptism is based on 1 Peter 3:20–21, where the salvation of Noah by the water of the flood is explained as a "figure" of baptism: "Wherein [that is, in the ark] few, that is, eight souls were saved by water. The like figure whereunto even baptism doth also now save us (not the putting away of the filth of the flesh, but the answer of a good conscience toward God)."

There is nothing in 1 Peter 3 of a common grace preservation of Noah and the human race from the peril of physical destruction and in mere earthly life, as is the teaching of Kuyper. Worthy of special note, against Kuyper's explanation of the salvation of Noah in the ark, is that 1 Peter 3 does not state that Noah and his family were saved *from* the flood. Rather, they were saved "*by* water." Regarding that Old Testament type, the water of the flood saved Noah spiritually from the wicked world of ungodly humans and their culture.

Regarding the New Testament reality, the blood of Christ saves believing parents and their children from the guilt and pollution of sin.

An argument that Kuyper thought was strong, if not decisive, against this explanation of the salvation of the flood was that one of those who were saved in the ark was a reprobate. Kuyper argued that the salvation in the ark cannot be explained as typical of spiritual salvation by the blood of Christ because Noah's son Ham was a reprobate.

> The "grace" displayed in the flood was not *special* grace but *common* grace. The ark did not save unto eternal life but for temporal life on earth. This explains how in the ark not only the "church of God" was rescued but also the reprobate Ham, together with the animals.[14]

Kuyper's argument explaining the flood as merely a physical deliverance and viewing the covenant with Noah as merely a covenant of common grace, because Ham was reprobate, fails by virtue of the fact that Ham was not a reprobate but one of God's elect. Scripture records a gross sin of Ham after the flood, even as it records a gross sin of Noah. These sins, however, do not prove the reprobation of either of them. The sins only show that the salvation of Noah and his family by the flood, in the ark, was a type, not the reality.

But scripture reveals that all eight saved in the ark, including Ham, were elect, believing, saved children of God. According to 1 Peter 3:20–21, "Eight souls were saved by water," with a salvation whereunto baptism is now a type, saving us with the spiritual salvation that is in the risen Christ. Second Peter 2:5 teaches that all eight persons in the ark were saved with the same salvation that saved Noah, and that salvation was spiritual in its nature and typology. Hebrews 11:7 proclaims that the faith of Noah was the means of the saving of his house, including Ham. That salvation was the spiritual salvation of being "heir of the righteousness which is by faith."

---

14 Ibid., 110.

Condemning Ham as a reprobate gains traction from the unspoken assumption that Noah cursed Ham for his sin of not privately covering Noah's nakedness and thus covering his sin. But the Bible never says that Noah cursed Ham. Rather, Noah cursed Ham's son Canaan (Gen. 9:25), who was not one of those saved in the ark but was born later.

The Cosmic Character of the Covenant with Noah

The covenant with Noah after the flood, as recorded in Genesis 9, was a particular, grand revelation of God's one covenant of grace with Jesus Christ and all those humans who are in him by a true faith, according to God's eternal decree of election. It was an extraordinarily important and glorious revelation of the one covenant of grace of God in Jesus Christ. Not only is Kuyper's explanation of the Noahic covenant as a covenant of common grace mistaken, with grievous consequences for Reformed theology and for the life of Reformed church members, but Kuyper's explanation also strips the covenant of grace in Christ Jesus of no small part of its truth and glory.

God's covenant of grace in Jesus Christ is with the entire human race—with Noah and his sons, from whom come all nations. But as Paul explains concerning the nation of Israel in Romans 9–11, in the reckoning of God the race is not every individual without exception. The genuine human race consists of the elect in Christ in every nation, tongue, and tribe. As the elect among them are the true Israel, so the elect among them are the true Dutch, the true Russians, the true Filipinos, and the true Chinese. These are "the nations of them which are saved," who will inherit the new world. The elect among all nations "shall bring the glory and honor of the nations into" the holy city, new Jerusalem (Rev. 21:24, 26). As Revelation 21:27 explicitly states, the nations that will inherit the new world, of which the world after the flood was a type or figure, do not consist of those who defile, work abomination, or make a lie. They consist of those "written in the Lamb's book of life," which is eternal election.

Included in the salvation of the covenant of God in Jesus Christ is the earth itself and its various creatures, particularly the animals. The covenant with Noah expressly includes the animal world: "the fowl...cattle...every beast of the earth" (Gen. 9:10). From this inclusion of animals, Kuyper and his disciples conclude that the covenant with Noah cannot have been a revelation of the covenant of (special) grace in Jesus Christ. This is a mistake.

Reference to all nations and even to animals does not prove the covenant with Noah to have been a different covenant from the covenant with the elect church in Jesus Christ. Rather, this reference makes known the expansive nature of the one covenant of grace in Jesus Christ.

Already the Old Testament disabuses the advocates of a covenant of common grace with Noah of their assumption that a covenant that includes animals cannot be the covenant of grace in Jesus Christ. Isaiah prophesied the coming perfected kingdom of the Messiah ("a root of Jesse" [Isa. 11:10]) as an earth in which "the wolf also shall dwell with the lamb, and the leopard shall lie down with the kid; and the calf and the young lion and the fatling together...and the cow and the bear shall feed; their young ones shall lie down together: and the lion shall eat straw like the ox" (vv. 6–7). Isaiah 65:25 repeats that when God creates a new heaven and a new earth (v. 17), "the wolf and the lamb shall feed together, and the lion shall eat straw like the bullock" in that new creation.

Contrary to Kuyper and his common grace disciples, the New Testament finds the fulfillment of the covenant with Noah, in all its breadth and scope, in the saving, covenantal work of Jesus Christ, the mediator of the covenant of (particular) grace. "God so loved the world" (John 3:16). In the Greek original, the word translated "world" is *kosmos* (cosmos), which word all are familiar with as referring to the universe. The reference in John 3:16 is to the whole of the creation that God made in the beginning, but not as made for Adam and having Adam as its head. Rather, as Colossians 1:16 teaches, the reference in John 3:16 is to the creation as made by and for Jesus Christ. "God so loved the world [cosmos], that he gave his only begotten Son." The explanation of God's gift of his Son as Savior is not only his love for humans, that is, the elect among all nations. The explanation includes as well the creation itself, the heavens and the earth, and the various creatures that inhabit the earth, particularly the animals.

The outstanding New Testament application and explanation of the covenant with Noah after the flood, however, is Romans 8:19–22:

19. For the earnest expectation of the creature waiteth for the manifestation of the sons of God.

20. For the creature was made subject to vanity, not willingly, but by reason of him who hath subjected the same in hope,

21. Because the creature itself also shall be delivered from the bondage of corruption into the glorious liberty of the children of God.

22. For we know that the whole creation groaneth and travaileth in pain together until now.

Throughout the passage, the word translated "creature" in verses 19–21 is the same word that is rightly translated "creation" in verse 22. The entire passage is glorious, staggering revelation concerning the future of the whole creation that God made in the beginning, as recorded in Genesis 1–2. The passage is revelation concerning the creation's sharing in the salvation of Jesus Christ crucified and risen, by the power of his Holy Spirit.

Particularly the earthly creation shares in the redemption of the cross. The risen Lord Jesus will one day renew this earthly creation by his Spirit. Then it will be purified of all the shameful filth with which it has been corrupted by the sinfulness of the human race. It will become the holy dwelling of the new, holy human race of which Jesus Christ is head. This is the future of the creation as the fullest and widest extension of the redemption of the cross and of the renewal of all things by the Spirit of Jesus Christ.

We elect believers look for and haste "unto the coming of the day of God, wherein the heavens being on fire shall be dissolved, and the elements shall melt with fervent heat." The fire that dissolves and melts the present form of the creation does not, however, annihilate the present creation. Out of the fire will come "new heavens and a new earth, wherein dwelleth righteousness" (2 Pet. 3:12–13).

Included in God's saving work in Jesus Christ is the present creation of heavens and earth. This salvation of the creation is part of the deliverance and renewal that belong to the covenant and covenantal salvation of God in Jesus Christ. Creation in Paul's day was not waiting in expectancy of the manifestation of Kuyper's common grace. It was waiting for the manifestation of the children of God by the special, saving grace of God in Jesus Christ. The hope of the creation is not that it will be delivered from the bondage of corruption into the partial, imperfect, inglorious liberty of Kuyper's common grace. The hope of the creation is that it will share, in a way fitting for the creation, in the liberty of the glory of the children of God, which is a liberty acquired by the cross and resurrection of Jesus Christ and a liberty accomplished by the Spirit of the crucified and risen Savior.

Creation is not presently groaning in expectation of rebirth as a creation by the efforts of Reformed theologians and of the Acton Institute in the power of Kuyperian common grace. It is groaning and travailing in eager expectation of its renewal by the crucified and risen Jesus Christ, in the power of his almighty, savingly gracious Spirit.

There are not two covenants and two kinds of salvation, side by side, one of saving grace in Jesus Christ and the other of common grace apart from Jesus Christ. There is one covenant with one salvation: the covenant of God of redeeming, saving, glorifying grace in Jesus Christ, extending not only to (elect) humans out of all nations, but also to the creation itself, as the dwellingplace of God with his human family.

Not only does Kuyper's theory of common grace miserably misconceive the covenant with Noah, it also miserably underestimates the salvation God has accomplished and will realize by his particular, saving grace in Jesus Christ. God's salvation in Jesus Christ is *cosmic*.

The covenant with Noah was so fundamental to Kuyper's theory of Christianizing the Netherlands and the world by a common grace of God that the exposure of Kuyper's explanation of that covenant demolishes his project of Christianizing the world. Indeed, with his explanation of the covenant with Noah falls the whole of Kuyper's theology of common grace.

CHAPTER 6

Reformed Critique of Kuyper's Common Grace Worldview: Scripture (2)

Colossians 1:13–20

One other passage in the New Testament was of vital importance to Abraham Kuyper with regard to his theory of common grace: Colossians 1:13–20.[1] In this marvelous passage, the apostle of Jesus Christ fairly outlines, as nowhere else in the Bible so clearly and fully, the one, vast, grand Christian worldview. In the passage, the apostle declares that God's "dear Son" (v. 13), who is "the Lord Jesus Christ" (v. 2), is "before all things" (v. 17) and is the end or goal of all things ("all things were created...for him," v. 16). That is, the whole of creation was brought into being by God with Jesus in view and for his sake. It was eternally God's purpose with "all things" that they serve Jesus Christ, so that "in all things he might have the preeminence" (v. 18). It was the pleasure of the Father with the entire creation that he made in the beginning "that in him [the Lord Jesus Christ] should all fulness dwell" (v. 19). This pleasure and purpose of God with the entire creation are realized by Christ Jesus' reconciling "all things unto himself; by him, I say, whether they be things in earth, or things in heaven" (v. 20).

---

1   James D. Bratt asserts that Colossians 1:13–20 is the *"locus classicus"* of Kuyper's theory of common grace (*Abraham Kuyper: A Centennial Reader*, 186).

This reconciling of all things to Jesus Christ, and to God in him, does not take place, nor is God's intention that it take place, by some common grace, merely outward Christianizing of all things, but by "the blood of his cross" (v. 20). "The blood of his cross" is, bespeaks, and carries out the reconciling, uniting, glorifying power of the (one) special, particular, redeeming grace of God.

This passage represented a serious, indeed fatal, problem for the common grace theory of Kuyper. The problem posed by the passage for Kuyper then and for all his common grace disciples today is this. First, Kuyper posited two distinct worldviews—I may say, by way of clarification, two distinct purposes of God with creation and its history: the salvation of the church by special grace and the cultural development of the creation by common grace. But Colossians 1 clearly teaches *one* worldview—one purpose of God with creation and history, which includes the redemption of the church at the very core of this one purpose. This one purpose of God with all things is realized in, by, and for Jesus Christ by the special (not common), saving (not cultural) grace expressed by the "blood of his cross."

The second problem for Kuyper was that, whereas Kuyper taught a preservation and development of the creation ("all things") *apart from* and *alongside* Jesus Christ, Colossians 1 explicitly teaches that God's one purpose with everything is that "in all things [the Lord Jesus Christ] might have the preeminence" (v. 18).

To his credit, Kuyper faced his problem forthrightly. However, he solved it wrongly. Realizing that two completely different, separate, and independent worldviews are unsatisfactory, indeed intrinsically contradictory of the very concept of worldview and therefore absurd, Kuyper tried to bring the common grace worldview and the particular grace worldview together in Christ, in light of Colossians 1.

Kuyper maintained the worldview of common grace as a "totally other work of God" than his work of special (saving) grace.

There is beside the great work of God in *special* grace also that totally other work of God in the realm of *common* grace...[This is] the great work that God is doing to consummate the world's development. And though a great deal in all this *we* cannot connect with the Kingdom or the content of our faith, nevertheless it all has meaning.[2]

Now the challenge was somehow to relate the two different works of God in history so that they might form a unified worldview and to relate them somehow in Christ, as Colossians 1 demands.

Having differentiated the work of God by special grace from "that totally other work of God in the realm of *common* grace," Kuyper exerted himself to relate the two works of God. But he brought the two different purposes of God together this way: the common grace development of the world takes place by and for the sake of not the man Jesus, but the second person of the Trinity. On the other hand, the purpose of God with saving, particular grace takes place by and for the sake of the incarnate Son of God, Jesus the Christ. Thus there is a kind of unifying of the two purposes of God with creation and history. The unity is the oneness of Jesus, who is both the eternal Son of God and a human. "The self-same Christ is simultaneously two things: the root of the life of creation as well as the root of the life of the new creation."[3]

Compelled by Colossians 1:13–20, Kuyper had to explain the relation, the unity, of the "work of creation and the work of redemption" in his theology of common grace, which for Kuyper amounted to the relation, the unity, of "the work of common and of special grace."[4] This "unity," Kuyper affirmed, is "in Christ only." But the Christ who is the unity of the two "totally" different works of God is not the incarnate Son of God, Jesus. Rather, he is "the eternal Son of God."

---

2   Kuyper, "Common Grace," in Bratt, *Abraham Kuyper: A Centennial Reader*, 176; emphasis is Kuyper's.

3   Ibid., 186.

4   Ibid., 184–85.

It must again get through to the Reformed mind that the work of creation and the work of redemption—and to that extent also the work of common and of special grace—find a higher unity in Christ *only because the eternal Son of God is behind both starting points.*[5]

"Starting points," of course, refer to the principles of God's two different works, that of common grace and that of special grace.

So committed was Kuyper to the "totally other work of common grace" that in the very same sentence in which he located the unity of the two works of God in the eternal Son of God Kuyper concluded that "the two operations [the work of common grace and the work of special grace] *diverge.*"[6] Despite their formal unity in the eternal Son of God, the works of common grace and of special grace are "totally other" works of God in history after all. They "diverge."

But it is Kuyper's attempt to unify the two works of God in history that concerns us and that ought to concern every Reformed church that is under the influence of Kuyper's common grace theory. Sharply differentiating the eternal Son of God from Jesus, the virgin-born, crucified, and risen Son of God in human flesh, Kuyper asserts that in Colossians 1:13–20 it was the eternal Son of God who created all things in the beginning. It was "not 'the human being Jesus Christ' [who] created the world."[7] Accordingly, the eternal Son of God, not the man Jesus, controls the development of creation in history. This development, of course, is for Kuyper the cultural development of history by the power of God's common grace. Not Jesus Christ but "the Son of God...determines the plan of the world."[8]

---

5 Ibid.; emphasis added.

6 Ibid., 185; emphasis added.

7 Ibid.

8 Ibid. Kuyper returned to Colossians 1:13-20 and his differentiation of the eternal Son from Christ Jesus in the third volume of his *Gemeene Gratie*, the practical part. Here he relates the eternal Son to the state, whereas Jesus Christ is related to the church. Once again, Kuyper asserts that "particular grace presupposes common grace" (120). For Kuyper's full argument on behalf of the distinction between the second person of the Trinity and Jesus the Christ, see pages 118-21.

In differentiating Christ as the eternal Son from Christ as incarnate, in the interests of his theory of common grace, Kuyper went so far as to ridicule the confession that the Creator of the world was the eternal Son *as the one who would become incarnate as the man Jesus.* Kuyper mocked the Reformed thinking that

> focused the divine powers of the Eternal Logos on the "holy child Jesus" in his human manifestation. In reference to the cradle of Bethlehem it delighted to exhaust itself in high-flown rhetorical linkages that applied the attributes of the Creator to that which is creaturely in the Savior. That "Infant in the cradle" had created the world; that "Infant in the cradle" upheld the world; and before long, in its view, the God who carried the world died in Jesus on the cross.

Such thinking, according to Kuyper, at best amounts to a "magic show." At worst, it is guilty of "lapsing into creature-worship."[9]

In thus severely criticizing Reformed preachers for doing justice in their sermons to the relation of the divine and human perfections in the person of the man Jesus, Kuyper evidently forgot the revelation of scripture, which does not so hermetically seal off the perfections of the eternal person of Jesus the Christ from the man, and even the baby, Jesus. Is it high-flown rhetoric that the wise men worshipped the baby Jesus in the cradle as God himself (Matt. 2:2, 11)? Is it high-flown rhetoric that of the Word made flesh, as he dwelt among us as the man Jesus and whose glory therefore we saw, John 1:14 declares that his glory, which we saw, is the glory of the only begotten of the Father? Is it high-flown rhetoric in John 1:3 to state of this Word become flesh in Jesus that he made the world? Is it even high-flown rhetoric when the apostle of Jesus Christ preaches that in the crucifixion of the man Jesus God himself "purchased [the church] with his own blood" (Acts 20:28)?

---

9   Ibid., 183. That Kuyper should criticize other theologians for "high-flown rhetoric" defies belief.

In distinction from the eternal Son of God, Kuyper continued, it is the Son of God incarnate, the man Jesus, in Colossians 1:13–20 who made peace through the blood of the cross, thus redeeming the elect church.

Although ostensibly discovering the unity of God's two works in history in the person of the eternal Son, Kuyper in fact promotes division and difference. Now the division and difference are thrust back into the very being and work of the eternal Son of God. As the eternal Son, according to his person, he is the "Mediator of creation." As the eternal Son in human flesh, according to the incarnation, he is the "Mediator of sinners." Furthermore, Christ's being the "Mediator of creation" has precedence over his being the "Mediator of sinners."

> Not first the Mediator of redemption and now, to achieve that role, also admitted as the Mediator of creation. But rather, first the original Mediator of creation and after that also the Mediator of redemption to make possible the enforcement and fulfillment of the decree of creation and everything entailed in it.[10]

What this means for his theory of common grace—and in all this theological speculation Kuyper is avowedly defending his theory of common grace, attempting to square it with Colossians 1:13–20—is that God has two distinct and different purposes with history. The first is the development of culture by all the human race, reprobate and elect alike. This purpose God realizes by the eternal Son, who is not incarnate in the man Jesus, and therefore God realizes this purpose apart from the cross and resurrection of Jesus Christ. The power of realizing this purpose is common grace: "Christ is the root of creation and therefore of common grace."[11]

The second purpose of God with history is the redemption of an elect church out of the nations. This purpose God realizes by the incarnate Son, the man Jesus. The power of realizing

---

10 Ibid., 185.

11 Ibid., 186.

this purpose is special (saving) grace: "Christ is...also the root of the life of the new creation or of special grace."[12]

Such is the importance of the common grace purpose of God with history, by the eternal Son simply in his divine person, that the work of special grace, by the incarnate Son, Jesus, serves the fulfillment of the purpose of God with common grace. The Christ of redemption is subservient to the Christ of creation. "The Mediator of redemption...make[s] possible the enforcement and fulfillment of the decree of creation and everything entailed in it."[13]

The grand work of special grace, involving the wonder of the incarnation, the mystery of the cross—"My God, my God, why hast thou forsaken me?"—and the glory of the resurrection, ascension, sitting at the right hand of God, and outpouring of the Spirit, takes a back seat to the project of common grace, which project does not involve the incarnate Son and his work of glorifying the Father who sent him. This is a disparagement of Jesus Christ, the incarnate Son, that no Reformed church, theologian, or believer should countenance for one moment.

The apostle was resolved to know nothing "save Jesus Christ, and him crucified" (1 Cor. 2:2). Kuyper and his contemporary disciples are determined to know something else than Jesus Christ, something else that is quite beside Jesus Christ, something else that is more important both to God and to them. The Protestant Reformed Churches demur.

The Worldview of the "Firstborn of Every Creature"

This ingenious effort by Kuyper to save his theory of the worldview of common grace in the face of the testimony of Colossians 1:13–20 comes to naught by two grievous, and obvious, errors. First, Kuyper's explanation of the two

---

12   Ibid., 187.

13   Ibid., 185.

purposes of God with history, amounting to two independent worldviews, leaves the two purposes of God—the two worldviews—*separate* from each other, not only distinct, but also unrelated. The cultural purpose of God, achieved by common grace, is carried out by and for the second person of the Trinity, who is not incarnate in the man Jesus. The saving purpose of God, achieved by particular, or special, grace, is carried out by and for the incarnate Son, the man Jesus.

What the relation between the two purposes of God—the two worldviews—might be, Kuyper does not tell us. It is not enough merely to affirm that "the work of creation and the work of redemption...find a higher unity in Christ" as the eternal Son of God.[14] It is not enough merely to assert that, accordingly, "there is thus no doubt whatever that common grace and special grace come most intimately connected from their origin, and this connection lies in Christ [as the eternal Son]."[15]

Kuyper must instruct his followers and readers what this connection actually is. He must explain the oneness of a worldview of common grace and of a worldview of special grace that have the eternal Son of God busy with two "totally" different activities in history, realizing two different purposes of God with history. He must indicate the actual unity of purpose and work of the eternal Son of God's fulfilling a purpose of God regarding creation by common grace and of the eternal Son of God in human flesh, the man Jesus', fulfilling the purpose of God to redeem a church by special grace.

Kuyper must set forth this unity because doing so is essential to worldview. Kuyper must set forth this unity because Colossians 1:13–20 is divine revelation of the (unified) worldview that the Kuyper of common grace urges upon his Reformed followers, then and now. And Kuyper must set forth this unity not by the exercise of his own ingenuity,

---

14   Ibid., 184–85.

15   Ibid., 187.

but in strict accordance with the binding truth of Colossians 1:13–20. This explanation, Kuyper fails to give. He contents himself with mere assertion.

The second grievous error of Kuyper's defense of his common grace worldview in light of Colossians 1:13–20 is simply but profoundly this, that the entire Colossians passage is about the "dear Son [of God]: in whom we have redemption through his blood" (vv. 13–14). That is, the subject of the entire passage, in every respect, is the eternal Son of God *as incarnate in the man Jesus the Christ*. The subject is not the eternal Son in himself but the eternal Son as "the firstborn of every creature" (v. 15). The eternal Son simply as the eternal Son is not the firstborn of every creature. As the eternal Son in and by himself, he does not belong to the category of creature, whether as firstborn or any other "born." As the eternal Son, he is the creator. Only as incarnate, in the man Jesus, is the eternal Son the "firstborn of every creature."

This determines the meaning of all of Colossians 1:13–20. This sets forth plainly and gloriously the one, only, and unified Christian worldview. This reveals the only worldview that may appeal to Reformed theologians, churches, and members in the twenty-first century. Essentially the unity of the worldview of God, which ought also to be ours, is Jesus the Christ, as the incarnate Son of God, who accomplishes God's one, grand purpose by particular, saving grace, to which all God's almighty and everywhere-present power of providence, now in the hands of the risen Jesus, is subservient.

This demolishes the common grace worldview of Kuyper in his day and of his disciples today, with its purpose for creation and history apart from God's dear Son *in our flesh*, the man Jesus. With the demolition of this worldview is doomed the project of common grace, namely, Christianizing the world.

For Jesus, "all things were created" (v. 16).

"It pleased the Father that in [Jesus] should all fulness dwell," because God eternally decreed "that in all things [Jesus] might have the preeminence" (vv. 18–19). "All things" include the whole of creation and the entirety of history, what Kuyper and his disciples refer to as culture and the products of culture.

By Jesus, God has reconciled "all things unto himself... whether they be things in earth, or things in heaven" (v. 20).

Nor does the creation of all things ignore Jesus in favor of the eternal Son simply as divine, altogether apart from his incarnation as the man Jesus. Conclusively against this notion stands the plain text of Colossians 1:13–20, particularly verses 13–17. "By him," that is, by God's "dear Son: in whom we have redemption through his blood" and who is "the firstborn of every creature"—"by him were all things created, that are in heaven, and that are in earth, visible and invisible, whether they be thrones, or dominions, or principalities, or powers: all things were created by him," as well as "for him." "He," that is, the incarnate Son, Jesus, "is before all things, and by him all things consist."

As verses 18–20 go on to teach, he who created the universe is the one who is the head of the church and who reconciled all things to God "through the blood of his cross."

Kuyper's prodigious effort to differentiate the eternal Son, who created all (on behalf of a cultural work of common grace), from the incarnate Son, who redeems by special grace, opposes the clear, powerful insistence of scripture in the passage that the creator and the redeemer is one and the same, and that this one is the incarnate Son of God, whose name is Jesus.

It is true, of course, and this is the force of Kuyper's superficial argument that our explanation of Colossians 1:13–20 must distinguish the eternal Son from the man Jesus, that Jesus was not yet born when God created all things in the beginning. When Colossians 1:13–20 declares that all things were created by "the firstborn of every creature," who is Jesus, it teaches that the person of Jesus is the person of the eternal Son of God. The Son, who would become flesh in Jesus in the fullness of time, created all things with the Father and the Holy Ghost.

But this is by no means all that the Holy Ghost taught when he inspired Colossians 1:13–20, particularly verse 16. This is not even the main thing that the Holy Ghost taught. The main thing is that in the beginning of Genesis 1, when the eternal Son created all things, he created all things *as the one who by divine decree, including his own decree, would become the man Jesus.* Not simply in his divine being did he create all things, but in his divine being *as determined to become incarnate* did he create all things. Thus, in truth and reality, all things were created by him whose name is Jesus.

The *Logos* (Word) of John 1:1–3, who made all things, is this *Logos* as the one who would be made flesh in the fullness of time (John 1:14), that is, as Jesus. The creator of the universe is therefore Jesus the Christ, the incarnate Son of God.

This is what the Heidelberg Catechism teaches when it attributes the creation of the universe not to the triune God but to "the eternal Father of our Lord Jesus Christ" and when, in the same Lord's Day, it goes on to describe the one who "upholds and governs" the creation as the believer's God and Father "for the sake of Christ his Son."[16] The creator is not simply God, or the triune God, but the Father of our Lord Jesus Christ. The God of providence is not simply God, but God as he is my God and my Father for the sake of Christ.

With the Bible, particularly Colossians 1:13–20, we are to know nothing save Jesus, whether regarding redemption or creation, whether regarding church history or secular history, whether regarding worship or culture, whether regarding Martin Luther and the sixteenth-century Reformation of the church or Abraham Lincoln and the Civil War.

Thus Jesus made all things in the beginning. Thus by Jesus do all things consist. Thus Jesus is before all things. Thus in all things Jesus has the preeminence, according to the pleasure of the Father that in Jesus should all fullness dwell.

Contrary to Kuyper and his common grace disciples, the worldview—not worldviews (plural)—of Colossians 1:13–20

---

16 Heidelberg Catechism Q&A 26, in Schaff, *Creeds of Christendom*, 3:315.

is this. The triune God eternally determined to glorify himself by the incarnate Son, Jesus the Christ. The unity of the (one and only, unified) Christian, and Reformed, worldview, as determined by God, is Jesus. By Jesus and for Jesus all things were created in the beginning. Creation and history, with every creature and regarding every event, exist and take place for the sake of Jesus. Nothing exists and nothing has ever happened except for the sake of Jesus. This includes the institution of marriage on the sixth day of the creation week; the fall of the race into sin shortly thereafter; the rise of Babylon as a world power; the existence of Judas Iscariot; some obscure carpenter who made crosses about AD 33; the present moral and ethical decline of the United States; the rising of the sun this morning; and the falling of a sparrow from a housetop.

That we cannot comprehend how everything serves Jesus Christ is not strange. God's ways are deep and mysterious. The confession of biblical worldview is a matter not of our comprehension but of our faith. Concerning God's government of history by his providential power and wisdom, the Belgic Confession has the Reformed Christian freely acknowledge:

> And as to what he doth surpassing human understanding we will not curiously inquire into it further than our capacity will admit of; but with the greatest humility and reverence adore the righteous judgments of God which are hid from us, contenting ourselves that we are disciples of Christ, to learn only those things which he has revealed to us in his Word without transgressing these limits.[17]

God does not yet reveal to the church and her members *how* all things relate to Jesus Christ and serve him. But he does assure the church *that* all things are related to Jesus Christ and serve him. This assurance invariably includes the honoring and comforting of God's church on earth,

---

17 Belgic Confession 13, in ibid., 3:397.

that all things serve the welfare of the church, a truth that Kuyper ridiculed.

21. For all things are yours;

22. Whether Paul, or Apollos, or Cephas, or the world, or life, or death, or things present, or things to come; all are yours;

23. And ye are Christ's; and Christ is God's. (1 Cor. 3:21–23)

Because all things of creation and history, including culture, are ours for the sake of Jesus Christ, the church and her members are assured by the word of God that "all things work together for good to them that love God, to them who are the called according to his purpose" (Rom. 8:28). Not only are theological things related to the church, for example, the Council of Nicea, but also "all things" have their reason for existence in the being and welfare of the church, for example, in Paul's day, the emperor Nero and his persecution of the church. Not only do ecclesiastical things serve the church, but also "all things" work together for the good of the church and her members.

All things! The whole of creation, from the sun and its rising to the lily of the field and how it grows! The totality of history, including the massive development of godlessness and perversity of our time and the falling of a sparrow from a housetop!

This is the Reformed worldview, Kuyper and his defenders notwithstanding. It is the worldview that honors Jesus the Christ, as the incarnate Son of God, crucified, risen, governing all at the right hand of God with all the power of the God-head, and coming again to subdue all things to himself and thus to the triune God. It is the worldview that confesses the sovereignty and wisdom of God in the realizing of itself. And it is the worldview of the one, particular, special, reconciling, saving grace of God in Jesus Christ, accompanied by the wrath of God burning against the children of disobedience.

What is there of worldview that this view of the world lacks? Who can demonstrate that this worldview is not grounded in scripture and the Reformed creeds? How dare confessing Reformed Christians, beginning with Kuyper, slander this worldview as "Anabaptism"?

This is the worldview of Colossians 1:13–20: Jesus is the "firstborn of every creature."

A Christless Christianizing

Colossians 1:13–20 destroys the entire common grace theory and project of a Christianizing of the world apart from faith in, subjection to, and honoring of Jesus Christ by the vast majority of those supposedly doing the Christianizing. Common grace's Christianizing of the world ignores and leaves out the Christ, who is Jesus! One would think that even the simplest Christian, to say nothing of the brilliant Kuyper and of the learned Reformed theologians now cooperating with the Roman Catholic Acton Institute, would immediately notice the incongruity, indeed the absurdity, even more the impossibility, of Christianizing *without the Christ*. It is as though one were to explain a large godly family without reference to the father and mother who raised the family in the fear of the Lord Jesus, whose instruction guides the life of the family, and whose influence determines the thinking and behavior of the family long after father and mother are dead.

But matters are still worse. The common grace project is rebellion against God. God has revealed that it is his pleasure "that in all things he [the firstborn from the dead, who is Jesus] might have the preeminence" (Col. 1:18). Kuyper's common grace theory and project maintain and develop most things, that is, things of history and culture, apart from Christ, indeed leaving Christ out of the theory and project.

Because Kuyper's theory and project of common grace leave Jesus Christ out, the project ends in the antichrist and his godless, antichristian kingdom. This charge, which is devastating, must not be dismissed as exaggeration or as mere implication. Kuyper himself acknowledged this consummation of his common grace project in so many words.

The result of common grace's Christianizing of the world will be antichrist and his antichristian world kingdom.

> The closing scene in the drama of common grace can be enacted only through the appearance on stage of the man of sin…[Common grace] leads to the most powerful manifestation of sin in history.[18]

"The appearance of the 'man of sin' will be caused precisely by the functioning of common grace."[19] Common grace produces the antichrist!

Calvin scholar James Bratt candidly describes Kuyper's admission that common grace ends in the antichrist as "new and troubling territory for some of his [Kuyper's] readers."[20] But this judgment upon Kuyper's theology of common grace is much too mild. That the supposedly divine work of common grace climaxes in antichrist exposes the theory as utterly false and reprehensible, if not blasphemous. The grace of God produces…*antichrist*! Antichrist—outstanding product in history of the (common) *grace of God*.

Kuyper's own declaration that common grace will produce and culminate in antichrist is certainly a reason why no Christian ought to participate in the project of common grace. To participate is to make oneself responsible for producing antichrist. The fully developed culture of common grace that so fascinates the Reformed community will be the kingdom of antichrist, the "Babylon" of Revelation 18 that our God detests. Granting Kuyper's theory that the kingdom of antichrist is indeed the full realization of the kingdom of common grace, upon this kingdom of common grace falls the wrath of God. From the Kuyperian kingdom of common grace, as the kingdom of antichrist, God's people have the calling to "come out of her," lest they be partakers of her sins and receive of her plagues.

18 Kuyper, "Common Grace," in Bratt, *Abraham Kuyper: A Centennial Reader*, 180-82.

19 Kuyper, *Common Grace: Abraham–Parousia*, 546.

20 James D. Bratt, in Kuyper, "Common Grace," in *Abraham Kuyper: A Centennial Reader*, 182.

In reality, rather than this Babylon having been built up by the (common) grace of God, God will throw her down with violence in his wrath (Rev. 18).

In the bizarre, blasphemous speculation of Kuyper that common grace ends in the antichrist is found a grain of truth. The theory and practice of common grace do, in fact, produce antichristian results in the churches and schools that commit themselves to the theory. This has become starkly evident already in the approximately one hundred years since Kuyper unleashed the theory of common grace upon the Reformed churches and set afoot the common grace program of cooperation with the world of the ungodly to Christianize the world.

The results are in. The results are plain for all to see. And the results are depraved and damnable.

Where are Kuyper's once-glorious Reformed Churches in the Netherlands today? What has become of them? Do they show the marks of true churches of Jesus Christ? Are they even Christian in the most elastic sense of that word? Can a denomination of churches that, in its constitution, explicitly approves and defends sodomite and lesbian relationships as holy and a denomination that tolerates avowed atheists in its ministry be regarded as Christian churches?

What is the spiritual condition, what is the Reformed, indeed the Christian, character of Kuyper's university—the Free—today, founded as it was in the muck of the theology of common grace? Kuyper himself advertised the corrupt foundation of the Free University. He chose as the symbol of the university the pagan goddess of wisdom, Minerva. She adorned the ceremonial mace of the university. "When the Free University was officially opened on October 20, 1880, the ceremonial mace of the new university had at its head a silver statue of Minerva, the Roman goddess of wisdom/reason."[21] Kuyper's defense of this choice of a symbol for a Reformed university in no way contradicts James Bratt's

---

21 Bolt, *Free Church, Holy Nation*, 73n224. For a picture of the Minerva mace, see Bratt, *Abraham Kuyper: A Centennial Reader*, 168.

judgment that the symbol expressed that "common grace provided the theological basis for Kuyper's educational... venture" at the Free University.[22]

Is there anything left of the Reformed faith and life in that school? Has the worldview of common grace allowed for any remnant whatever of the worldview of special, particular grace? Has the principle of common grace permitted even a residue of the principle of the antithesis to remain? Has Minerva graciously permitted anything of John Calvin to influence the instruction? Every Reformed theologian, minister, professor of theology, Christian school teacher, and well-read layman in North America knows the answers to these questions. Every Reformed believer in all the world who is attracted to the theory of common grace is duty bound to ask these questions and to learn the answers—and then to learn *from* the answers.

Likewise, what is the doctrinal and spiritual condition of the Christian Reformed Church in North America today? What has the doctrine of common grace that she adopted in 1924 done to that once-glorious church, heir of the *Doleantie* of 1886, of the Secession of 1834, and of the Reformation of 1517? Has the doctrine allowed her to become stronger in the Reformed faith of the Canons of Dordt? Has the doctrine of common grace permitted her even to retain the Reformed faith, for example, with regard to the account of creation in Genesis 1–2; with regard to the particularity of the atonement; with regard to eternal, sovereign, double predestination? Has the doctrine of common grace allowed her to resist the blandishments of the world of the ungodly, for example, in matters of intermarriages with unbelievers; of worldly amusements, including dancing; of the sanctity of holy marriage, by repudiation of divorce and remarriage; of the divine ordinances regarding the place and calling of men and women in marriage and in the church, specifically the holding of office in the church?

---

22 Bratt, *Abraham Kuyper: A Centennial Reader*, 168.

What is the strength of the commitment of Calvin College, the official college of the Christian Reformed Church, to the Reformed theology of the creeds and to a distinctively antithetical, Reformed, Christian life? Has the theory of common grace tended to Christianize the surrounding world in the United States, or even in Grand Rapids, Michigan, or has it tended to make the teaching and life promoted by Calvin College worldly? Does the college (of which I am a graduate and not an unthankful one) today even entertain the reality and importance of the antithesis? Or is it conformed to the world in thinking, for example, denial of the historicity of Genesis 1–3 and acceptance of evolutionary theory as the explanation of origins? And is it conformed to the world in behavior, for example, acceptance of homosexuality as a Christian way of life, ostensibly on behalf of influencing the world and cooperating with the world?

Why do the United Reformed Churches, which recently split from the Christian Reformed Church exactly over the disastrous, world-conforming effects of common grace, particularly the world's thinking about the relation of men and women with regard to women in church office—why do the United Reformed Churches refuse to acknowledge the root of the evil but instead themselves contend for common grace as vigorously as the Christian Reformed Church and now cooperate in spreading the destructive doctrine of common grace on behalf of the project of Christianizing the world? Among the supporters and promoters of the translation of Kuyper's work *Common Grace* on behalf of the Christianizing of America and then the world is Mid-America Reformed Seminary, one of the leading, if unofficial, seminaries of the United Reformed Churches.[23] Evidently, in all their struggles in the Christian Reformed Church and despite all the upheaval of a church split, the leaders and members of the United Reformed Churches have learned nothing.

---

23 Kuyper, *Common Grace: Noah–Adam*, xv.

The Kuyperian theory of common grace with the practice that accompanies it is ecclesiastical suicide! The proof is in the pudding.

CHAPTER 7

The Cultural Calling of the Christian

Anabaptist?

The alternative to their theory, charge the advocates of common grace, is the pernicious error of Anabaptism. The persistent charge against those who deny common grace and reject its project of Christianizing the world is that they are Anabaptists. This was Kuyper's own charge against those who opposed his common grace vision and project in the late nineteenth and early twentieth centuries in the Netherlands.

Already in the foreword to his three-volume work *Common Grace*, Kuyper was charging those who opposed his Christianizing of the world by a common grace of God with the evil of Anabaptism. As though this evil were the alternative to his endeavor to Christianize the world by common grace, Kuyper remarked that "every Anabaptist sect had systematically isolated itself from the world."[1] What he meant by Anabaptism, and what he wanted his readers to understand by the epithet, he made clear when he added, "Spiritual isolation and ecclesiastical isolation are equally anti-Reformed."[2] If one was not on board with Kuyper's common

---

1   Ibid., 5.

2   Ibid., 6.

grace project, he was lumped with the sect of the Anabaptists, systematically isolating himself from the world—a damning charge for a Reformed man or woman. Thus, of course, Kuyper was promoting his venture by silencing the opposition.

Nothing if not slavish disciples of the Kuyper of common grace in all aspects of Kuyper's theory and practice, the Christian Reformed Church blackened Herman Hoeksema with the charge of Anabaptism in the early 1920s. They have worn out the accusation against the Protestant Reformed Churches over the past ninety years.

What is meant by the charge—if it does not serve merely to substitute for sound argument and to render odious an opponent whom one cannot otherwise defeat by name-calling—is that the Protestant Reformed Churches separate themselves from the world of humanity and its way of life *physically.* "Anabaptism" in the common grace controversy is the charge of *isolation—physical* isolation. It is the accusation that the Protestant Reformed Churches so concentrate on spiritual life and activities as to ignore, if not to reject, normal, earthly pursuits. It is the charge that these churches deny that the calling of the Christian is to serve God *in* earthly life, *in* all the ordinances and institutions of earthly life, for example, marriage, family, work, recreation, and government, and *with* earthly possessions and gifts.

In the words of an old Dutch proverb, it is the charge that one's view and practice of the Christian life consist of *"met een boekje in een hoekje"* ("with a little [religious] book in a little [out-of-the-way] corner"). In the language of the Bible, those who deny common grace, charge the defenders of it, are guilty of abstaining from creatures and institutions that are good and nothing to be refused (1 Tim. 4:1–7), of attempting what Jesus described as going "out of the world" (John 17:15).

The charge of Anabaptism against those churches that deny common grace is false. The charge is completely false. Those who raise the charge in order to smear and destroy the theological foes of Kuyperian common grace are guilty of slander—the violation of the ninth commandment of the law of God: bearing false witness against their (Reformed) neighbor. The advocates of common grace may amuse themselves, and others, and may defend their bad cause by continuing to have recourse to the charge of Anabaptism, but they should be sobered by the warning of the Heidelberg Catechism that by this slander they bring down upon themselves "God's heavy wrath."[3]

I do not intend to defend the life of all Protestant Reformed people. I do not intend to defend my own life as a Reformed Christian. What I will do, very briefly, is expose the charge of "world flight," or Anabaptism, as false, regarding the application of these epithets to the doctrinal rejection of Kuyperian common grace by the Protestant Reformed Churches in America.

Rejection of common grace is not Anabaptism. Rejection of common grace has absolutely nothing to do with Anabaptism. Rejection of common grace is not inclined to lead to Anabaptism. The Protestant Reformed Churches are as opposed to Anabaptism as they are to common grace. The alternatives with regard to the active Christian life are not, and never have been, common grace and Anabaptism.

What is the authentic worldview of the Reformed faith? How do sound Reformed believers, without any Anabaptist tendencies, live the Reformed, Christian life, and why?

The Reformed Worldview

The soundly Reformed Christian believes, confesses, and practices a worldview. Much as he differs with Kuyper on the meaning and purpose of Kuyper's stirring statement in his address at the inauguration of the Free University in 1880, the Reformed believer is in agreement with the statement: "There is not a square inch in the whole domain of our human existence over which Christ, who is Sovereign over *all*, does not cry: 'Mine!'"[4]

---

3   Heidelberg Catechism Q 112, in Schaff, *Creeds of Christendom*, 3:348.

4   Kuyper, "Sphere Sovereignty," in Bratt, *Abraham Kuyper: A Centennial Reader*, 488.

The Reformed believer repudiates Anabaptist world flight. He neither preaches nor practices *"met een boekje in een hoekje,"* although he would find this better than *"met een TV in een hoekje."*

The Reformed, Christian, entire, earthly life is a sacred calling. It is to be lived in *any* or *all* of the ordinances or spheres of the earthly creation, for example, marriage, labor, and government. It consists of using and developing all of one's physical gifts and abilities, for example, music, scholarship, and motherhood. It not only allows, but also encourages enjoyment of all the legitimate beauties and pleasures of earthly life, whether a Van Ruisdael painting—"The Storm"—at the Louvre in Paris, or a Mozart symphony in Orchestra Hall in Chicago, or a glorious sunset over Lake Michigan, or simply a good steak dinner.

The Reformed Christian is permitted, indeed required, to live this godly life in physical contact and even earthly cooperation with the ungodly, for example, at work, in the neighborhood, and in the life of the nation.

In the world, Jesus taught in John 17:15. To avoid contact with the ungodly, the Reformed Christian would have to go out of the world, and the apostle forbids this in 1 Corinthians 5:10. Having forbidden the members of the congregation at Corinth to "company with fornicators" who have been excommunicated from the church (v. 9), the apostle quickly adds, "Yet not altogether with the fornicators of this world." If company with all fornicators of this world was forbidden, "then must ye needs go out of the world," and going out of the world is both impossible and contrary to the will of God for the life of his child.

Nothing human is off-limits to the Reformed Christian. Everything human is allowed to him or her. Much that is human is required of the Reformed Christian.

"Human," I say, with reference to our creaturehood, as made by God in the beginning. A great deal of *corrupted* human life is forbidden to the Reformed Christian: aborting unborn children; pornography; recreational drugs;

drunkenness; unbiblical divorce; the remarriage of divorced persons; sodomy and lesbianism.

Cooperation with the ungodly in *unlawful* human activities is forbidden to the Reformed believer: rebellion against the authority of the employer by the strike of labor unions; revolutionary acts against government, even though the government is unjust; promotion of same-sex "marriage."

Friendship with unbelievers is forbidden. Contact in everyday life is one thing. Friendship, which is communion of life, is another thing. Since the unbeliever is not one with the believer in Jesus Christ by the Holy Spirit and on the foundation of the word of God, fellowship of the believer with the unbeliever is both proscribed and impossible. On the contrary, the friend of God hates God's enemies (Ps. 139:21–22).

But this spiritual separation from and enmity toward the corrupt world of the ungodly by no means proscribes a full, active Christian life in God's creation and its ordinances.

If the justification and warrant of a full, active, culturally engaged Christian life are not common grace, what are they?

The world in which we live is God's creation, with all its spheres or ordinances and with all its various creatures. As God's creation, this world and human life in it are "good, and nothing to be refused, if it be received with thanksgiving" (1 Tim. 4:4). The fall into sin of the race in Adam brought the curse upon the earthly creation but did not defile the creation so as to render it inherently evil and therefore off-limits to the holy children of God. Wicked men and women defile every aspect of creation that they touch, use, and enjoy, *for themselves*. It is as if they touch everything with filthy hearts and hands, thus making everything they touch dirty in their own use of it. They do not defile the creation with regard to the right touching, using, and enjoying of it by the believer. Creation remains the good work and world of God.

This is one aspect of the warrant for the believer's full and free life in the earthly creation. This world is the good creation of God. This aspect of the justification of the

Christian's culturally active life in the world, let it be noted, has nothing whatever to do with any common grace of God. The goodness of the creature is due to God's work of creation in the beginning. The continuing goodness of creation is due to God's work of providence, upholding the good creation.

A second aspect of the legitimacy of the Reformed Christian's life in all the spheres and ordinances of the creation is that Jesus Christ has redeemed the earthly creation. Because Jesus Christ died for the earthly creation itself, as well as for the elect human race that inhabits the creation, "the creature itself also shall be delivered from the bondage of corruption into the glorious liberty of the children of God" (Rom. 8:21).

As redeemed by Jesus Christ, the entire creation of the heaven and the earth belongs to Jesus Christ. It is not Satan's, although he presently usurps authority over the earthly creation and its development by his malign control over much of the human race. Neither is the earthly creation with its various creatures the rightful property of the wicked who dominate the earthly creation, whether the godless Communists or the equally godless secularists of the West. As God decreed from eternity and as God determined during the six days in which he made it all, the creation is the rightful possession of the Lord Jesus.

Belonging to Jesus, the creation therefore is ours, who are Christ's holy nation and new human race by the sanctifying power of his Spirit. We Christians have the right to the creation and all its creatures and ordinances, its beauties, its pleasures, its riches. We are the only humans with right to the earthly creation, as we are also the only humans with the ability to use, enjoy, govern, and develop the creation properly, that is, to the glory of God and in accordance with his law for the creation and human life in it. All use of the creation, extending to the breathing of its air, by those outside of and against Jesus Christ is presumption and robbery.

Once again, neither does this aspect of the warrant of the Christian for the use of the world have anything to do with a common grace of God. Christ did not redeem the world in a common grace of God. Nor does he give the world to his people by virtue of common grace. Nor do Christians work with, use, and develop the creation by the power of a common grace of God.

A third aspect of the right and duty of the Reformed Christian to live in and work with the earthly creation is that God's will, plainly revealed in holy scripture, is that the Christian serve and glorify God *in* the world, not by fleeing the world; by behaving rightly *in* the ordinances of creation, not by ignoring them; and by the proper *use* of the creation and its creatures, not by abstaining from the creation as much as possible. The Christian calling corresponds to the calling God gave to Adam in paradise, that he cultivate and guard the garden (Gen. 2:15).

The separation—antithesis—between the Reformed Christian and the world of ungodly men and women and their way of life is spiritual, not physical. This is the fundamental difference between the Reformed worldview and the worldview of Anabaptism. Anabaptism preaches and practices *physical* separation, *physical* withdrawal, *physical* isolation. *In* the world but not *of* the world is the doctrine of Jesus in John 17:14–18. Physically, his disciples are in the world; spiritually, they are not of it.

Although the will of God for the earthly lives of his people during the present age is that they lead distinctively Christian lives in the world, amid the ungodly inhabitants, it is not the purpose of God that the holy lives of his people Christianize society. The very word is deceptive: truly to Christianize would be to make something *Christian*, that is, believing in, enlivened by, devoted and submissive to Jesus the Christ. Doing justice to the word itself, to Christianize is not merely to apply a veneer of Christianity; it is not merely an outward show of Christianity or of some aspects of Christianity. Nor is it even to accomplish some inner regard for Christ on the part of the ungodly (as though this were possible) without the new birth and the indwelling of the Spirit of Christ.

Christianizing by Christ Alone

The grand work of making all of human life in the creation Christian cannot be accomplished by us, and certainly not by our being agents of common grace. Jesus Christ will make the society of all redeemed, renewed humanity Christian when he comes again on this world's last day. From this society will be banished all the reprobate wicked and Satan with his demons, whose malignant will and mighty powers are underestimated by the advocates of the rosy optimism of common grace. Only Christ can lift the entire creation and all its inhabitants into the peace and glory of which the Kuyper of common grace dreamed, and Christ will perform the wonder only upon his return.

This renewal of the creation and making Christian the life of the race in the creation will not take place as a gradual improvement of the existing world and its inhabitants, as are the dream and program of Kuyper's disciples. But the renewal will occur by way of the catastrophic, fiery destruction of the present form of the creation (2 Pet. 3:10–13); by way of a public, final judgment that separates the sheep from the goats, banishing the goats from the new creation (Matt. 25:31–46); and by way of the resurrection of elect humanity into perfectly holy, sinless life (1 Cor. 15).

The love and power that will bring about the new world in which righteousness will finally dwell, and dwell forever (2 Pet. 3:13), are not those of any common grace. They will be the love and power that gave the eternal Son into human flesh; that nailed him to the cross; that raised him from the dead; and that alone can lift a sin-cursed world into the freedom and glory of the perfected kingdom of God, as they alone can make men and women who are by nature children of the devil sons and daughters of God. The love and power that alone can, and will, truly Christianize the world are the Holy Spirit of Jesus Christ, who operates by special grace—the grace of the crucified and risen Jesus Christ.

It is another offense of Kuyper's common grace that it virtually attributes to a grace of God apart from Jesus the

Christ the power and glory with which God has graced his Son in human flesh. The honor that belongs alone to Jesus Christ, God in the flesh, namely, the glory of making the world of the nations Christian, Kuyper and his disciples give to an alliance of sinful Calvinistic humans and the Roman Catholic Church, working altogether apart from the grace of the cross and of the resurrection of Jesus and therefore without the power of the Spirit of Jesus Christ. The theory of common grace is, throughout, a doctrine of salvation—*cosmic* salvation—apart from Christ Jesus. It is therefore non-Christian, if not anti-Christian.

God's will is that his redeemed people live a full, active earthly life in all the ordinances and with all their powers and talents. But God's purpose with our full, active Christian life on earth, in the creation ordinances, and using all the creatures and abilities that are at our disposal is not that we Christianize the world. If this is the purpose of God, his purpose has failed for the past two thousand years. It failed with regard to Kuyper and his followers in the Netherlands in the early 1900s. One thing Amsterdam and the whole of the (little) Netherlands are not, in 2016, is Christian.

The Christianizing of society has not been noticeably realized by the Christian Reformed Church and by its Calvin College over the past ninety years, not even in religious Grand Rapids, Michigan. As I write, the political, cultural, and even ecclesiastical powers in Grand Rapids are working with might and main to approve sodomite and lesbian sexual relations and even to legitimize them as forms of holy marriage, while demonizing the biblical condemnation of these perversities. If any city in North America should show the Christianizing effects of a common grace of God and thus substantiate the theory of common grace and its Christianizing project, Grand Rapids is this city.

Grand Rapids is the ecclesiastical, educational, and social center of the movement of common grace. These agencies, people, and powers have been working at the Christianizing of Grand Rapids for some ninety years. But Grand Rapids has not been Christianized. On the contrary, it is being "sodomized."

Significantly, little or nothing is heard in the public media from the enthusiasts of the Christianizing crusade condemning this powerful movement of sodomizing the city. On the contrary, there is good reason to believe that when the sodomites officially prevail, as they will, under the wrath of God that gives ungodly men and women over to this perversity, the advocates of common grace will approve the decision not only as the will of the majority, but also as a Christian action of "love for everyone." Thus common grace will again have shown itself to be not the Christianizing of a godless society but the heresy that makes the church worldly.

The purpose of God with the holy life of his church in the world has never been, and is not now, the making Christian of the cultural life of the society of ungodly men and women among whom the saints live and work. But the purpose of God with the Christian life of his people, the truly Christian life that consists of doing good out of thankful love to God for his salvation of them in Christ Jesus by the power of the sanctifying Spirit of Christ in their regenerated, believing hearts, is their glorifying of him. This glorifying of God by his Christian people consists of their being spiritual, ethical light that exposes the shameful, sinful darkness of the depraved society in which they shine as light in the world.

This shining light that is the holy life of the people of God does not change the darkness of the ungodly world into light. It does not even diminish the darkness of the godless world. It certainly does not attract the darkness to itself, so that the darkness will cooperate in friendship with the light in glorifying God, who is light and whose light the light of his people is. Rather, the light contrasts with that darkness. It exposes the darkness for the deep darkness that it is, by the contrast with the light. The shining light of truth and holiness that is the life and testimony of the people of God brings upon the church and the Christian the hatred and persecution of the world of wicked men and women, because the darkness of unbelief, of the lie, and of depravity hates the light of faith, of the truth, and of holiness.

What did Jesus foretell for his disciples because of their being in the world? Was it friendly relations with the world in a cooperative effort to realize something of Christianity in the cultural life of the world? Nothing of the kind! On the contrary, "the world hath hated them, because they are not of the world, even as I am not of the world" (John 17:14).

Such is the depravity of the world, such is the world's hatred for Jesus Christ as the full revelation of God, that only one quality and one act will gain its approval: friendliness toward and conformity to the world of the ungodly in things spiritual and moral, as well as in things cultural and political. The church and the Christian must show themselves as being *of* the world, as well as in the world. That is, to gain the world's friendship and cooperation a church must commit ecclesiastical suicide. It must conform itself to the world. This is the real working of common grace, as is the very nature of the theory and as experience both in Kuyper's Netherlands and in the Christian Reformed Church's North America proves.

Putting the best construction on Kuyper's famous dictum "no square inch...," those who put the dictum into practice must not expect the world's approval, much less the world's friendly cooperation. Rather, they must expect ridicule, hatred, and outright persecution. The totally depraved world hates Jesus Christ. It hates him as the revelation of the holiness of God his Father. When the holy God appeared in the world of the creation in such a form that the world of the ungodly could get their hands on him, they *crucified* him.

Against the theory of common grace stands the very heart of the Christian religion: the cross of Jesus Christ.

The hatred and enmity of the world of the ungodly against Christ in his church and in the lives of his people are exactly what we experience at present. What is the world's response to our confession of the doctrine of creation, by and for the Christ who is Jesus, as taught in Genesis 1–2, accompanied by our condemnation of the theory of evolution, as cultural a matter as could be imagined? What is the world's response to our doctrine and practice of marriage as a lifelong bond between one man and one woman, certainly a cultural matter? What is the world's response to our condemnation of homosexuality, also a cultural matter?

What is the world's response to our teaching about the authority of the owner of a business, including the duty of the laborer to submit, which forbids the strike, certainly a cultural matter? What is the world's response to our insistence on the calling of the wife to submit to the authority of her husband in marriage, obviously a cultural matter? What is the world's response to our prohibition of the citizenry of a nation to riot, again very definitely a cultural matter? What is the world's response to our judgment upon the welfare state in view of the biblical injunction that if a man will not work, neither shall he eat (2 Thess. 3:10), a cultural matter?

All of these positions of the true church of Christ in the world are concrete, biblical expressions of the truth that there is not one square inch in all creation about which Christ does not say, "Mine!" and over which he does not have authority. Do these stands of the church endear her to the world? Do they attract the world so that the world is willing to cooperate with the church in realizing these stands in our society? Do they enable the church to make common cause with the world in bringing about justice and order in society even outwardly?

Nothing of the sort! On the contrary, the homage that believers pay to Christ by their obedience to him in everyday, earthly life shows the deep and wide divide between the godly church and the ungodly world of unbelieving men and women. The more clearly the light of holiness shines in the lives of the people of God, the more intense is the hatred of the ungodly world.

Not only does the Kuyperian theory of common grace misconceive the purpose of the earthly lives of the godly, as though it were the Christianizing of the world, but it also errs greatly in its proposal of the power by which Reformed Christians are to live their godly, holy lives in all the earthly ordinances or spheres. Common grace proposes the feeble, indeed non-existent, power of a common grace of God.

If this grace existed, it could not serve as the energy of the Christian life in the world. It lacks the power to energize the glorious life of a Christian in a fallen, anti-Christian world. Common grace is, well, merely *common*. To live the Christian life, a man, a woman, a young person, a child need grace that is *special*, grace that is *extraordinary*, grace that is the power of Jesus Christ the incarnate Son of God risen from the dead, grace that is almighty and does wondrous things, because it is the life, energy, and power of the atoning death and victorious resurrection of Jesus.

According to Kuyper and his allies themselves, their common grace is not the power of the crucified and risen Son of God in human flesh, operating by and in the Spirit of Jesus Christ. Common grace therefore would be an inadequate power for the awesome calling of living the Christian life in the world.

All of his earthly life in the creation and its ordinances, regarding the use of all his gifts and abilities, the Reformed Christian lives by the power of the one, special, particular, saving grace of God in the risen Jesus Christ. He worships on the Lord's day by this one, mighty, glorious grace. He loves his wife and raises his children by this one, mighty, glorious grace. He tills his fields or builds and manages his business by this one, mighty, glorious grace. He labors in the factory to support his family and the church, in conscious obedience to the will of God his Father, or she manages her household, including cleaning dirty diapers, by this one, mighty, glorious grace. Indeed, such a mundane matter as eating and drinking he performs to the glory of God by this one, mighty, glorious grace.

This (special) grace is powerful. This grace glorifies God in all the earthly life of the believer. This grace stores up for him or her an everlasting reward for the Christianity of his or her life, whether in preaching good sermons or in changing the dirty diapers of God's needy, baptized, infant children. Did not Jesus encourage us that giving a cup of cold water in his name has its reward?

"*In his name!*" This name is not a name of common grace but the name of God's special grace. The implication is that to divorce virtually all of earthly life from special, saving grace is to divorce it from Jesus Christ himself. Those who do this will also have their reward, but this reward will not be pleasant.

Last Warning

I conclude with a warning.

There is something perverse about the emphasis in Reformed and evangelical circles today on avoiding the danger of Anabaptism, the danger of world flight. From the emphasis on the pressing need to avoid Anabaptism, one would get the impression that Anabaptism is the great threat of our day to the Reformed faith, to the Christian life, and to Christianity itself. The evil of world flight is apparently the great threat of the hour.

I am reminded of the observation by C. S. Lewis that humans, including Christians, are prone to the folly of warning against dangers that are no real threat, while ignoring the danger that seriously threatens. Lewis used the example of a crew and passengers on a sinking ship. Instead of calling for life rafts, they scream for fire extinguishers and run about the ship's deck spraying for fire.

The great threat to the church and to the Christian, particularly the Reformed church and the Reformed Christian, in our day is not world *flight* but world *conformity*. But the theologians warn at the top of their voices of the danger of world flight. They run about with fire extinguishers when they ought to be providing life rafts to Reformed Christians on sinking ships. Indeed, by the doctrine of common grace, these theologians add to the threat of the swallowing up of churches in the billowing waves of worldliness.

Still more, in the Bible are, I dare estimate, hundreds more warnings against worldliness than against the peril of world flight. "Be not conformed to this world" (Rom. 12:2). "Come out from among them, and be ye separate" (2 Cor. 6:17). "Ye adulterers and adulteresses, know ye not that the friendship of the world is enmity with God?" (James 4:4). These are merely an off-hand sampling of such warnings throughout the Bible. The whole history of Israel in the Old Testament is one extended warning against fellowship with, and being influenced by, the idolatrous world of the ungodly.

Where are these warnings today? They are seldom heard, and if heard only faintly, from the enthusiasts for common grace and cooperation with the world, to Christianize it.

In this book I sound the prominent biblical warning, and the Protestant Reformed Churches sound it always: "Come out from among them, and be ye separate." Regardless that this is not the warning given by the Reformed churches at the beginning of the twenty-first century, it is the warning of the Lord himself: "saith the Lord" (2 Cor. 6:17). God grant, in his "special" grace, that Reformed Christians hear and heed this warning!

In the way of our heeding the warning, and *only* in the way of our heeding the warning, that is, in the way of our living the antithesis, God himself declares, "I will receive you, and will be a Father unto you, and ye shall be my sons and daughters" (2 Cor. 6:17–18).

The way of common grace is a way of friendship with the world of the ungodly and therefore of enmity with God.

The way of special grace is the way of friendship with God and of enmity with his enemies.

INTRODUCTION TO PART 2

The lecture on Kuyper's theology of cultural common grace occasioned a number of questions from the audience. Time did not allow the answering of most of these questions at the public meeting itself. All of the questions and my answers to them are the content of what follows in this book.

Almost always, the question and answer period following a public lecture is an interesting, informative part of the gathering. Occasionally, this period is more interesting and informative than the speech itself. Whether this is the case regarding the content of this book is for the reader to decide.

In any case, these questions do in the main penetrate deeply into the subject of common grace and the Christianizing of culture, which was the topic of the lecture. The response to some of the questions expands on or grounds the content of the lecture.

These questions with their answers therefore are a valuable part of the book. They challenge the ardent advocates of common grace and its Christianizing crusade. They help those who struggle with the issue. They offer further support to those who take a stand against Kuyper's common grace theology as a recent, popular, serious weakening of the Reformed faith and life. They explain to the interested and concerned onlooker why the Protestant Reformed Churches dissent from the theology of common grace.

CHAPTER 8

Answers to Questions

(These questions were handed in by the audience after the lecture and are printed as they were written by those who asked them. The questions are printed in italics.)

1. How does your view of common grace relate to the sending out of missionaries by the church? Should we spread the gospel by distributing tracts, Bibles, and Christian literature at venues such as county fairs? In such instances, many are not likely to come to our churches, so should we not go to people there?

Kuyper's doctrine of common grace has nothing whatever to do with sending out missionaries or distributing literature. The grace of God that has to do with sending out missionaries and with distribution of Christian literature is a *saving* grace of God. Kuyper sharply distinguished his common grace from God's saving grace. Kuyper's common grace had only to do with culture and with improving human society. Kuyper warned against confusing his common grace with the saving grace of God, to the extent that he proposed two different names in Dutch for the two graces, as I pointed out in the lecture.

My condemnation of Kuyper's common grace does not at all imply a rejection of any and all lawful means to spread the gospel of salvation in Jesus Christ, including the church's sending out missionaries and an evangelism committee's distribution of tracts and pamphlets. But evangelism and missions are not activities on behalf of a common grace of God. They are means of the workings of God's (one) particular, saving grace.

2. Is common grace enough to save a person (so that he goes to heaven)?

According to Kuyper himself, common grace is not enough to save a person. Common grace is not *intended* by God to save anyone. Common grace is not able to save anyone. Common grace merely makes a person outwardly decent and moral, enabling him or her to live usefully and culturally productively in society and the nation.

However, as I noted in the lecture, Kuyper himself significantly weakened his own stand on this point by ascribing to common grace the power of creating in every human a "point of contact" for the gospel. Thus Kuyper himself, contrary to his own explicit warning, associated common grace with salvation. Even on this view, common grace by itself is not sufficient for salvation. For Kuyper, only particular, saving grace—the second kind of grace—saves humans.

3. How do Kuyper and Bavinck respond to the many times that Christ says that he prays not for the world but [only] for his people?

This question too, like some of the others, makes plain the difficulty, if not the impossibility, of sharply distinguishing between a non-saving, common grace of God and a saving, particular grace of God. When Reformed believers hear of a grace of God for humans, they conclude that that grace must be saving in nature and in purpose. Thus despite Kuyper's warnings that his common grace is fundamentally different from God's particular, saving grace, and despite Kuyper's intention sharply to distinguish common grace from particular grace, the Kuyperian doctrine of a common grace of God inevitably results in the belief of a saving grace of God that is universal, that is, the heresy of Arminianism that is condemned by the Canons of Dordt.

Learned theologians may be able to differentiate two distinct graces of God, although history casts doubt even on this. At its synod of 1924, the Christian Reformed Church, intending to make Kuyper's doctrine of common grace official church dogma and therefore binding upon one of its ministers, Rev. Herman Hoeksema, in fact adopted the gross false doctrine of a universal, ineffectual, saving grace of God—its well-meant offer of salvation.

The lay members of the churches certainly cannot distinguish two graces, one that is saving and the other that is non-saving. To the typical Reformed church member, grace is grace, and grace is saving. And the typical Reformed church member is right.

Kuyper and Bavinck would respond to this question by describing Christ's prayer on behalf of his elect people, for instance in John 17, as the expression of *particular, saving* grace. *Common* grace, they would say, and in fact did say, is only cultural, not saving. Common grace, which is cultural, is for all humans, reprobate as well as elect. Particular grace, which alone is saving, is for the elect only.

4. Would it be accurate to understand the real meaning of the charge "Anabaptist" against the Protestant Reformed Churches to mean that "they really don't go into the world" because they won't preach to the world that God loves all men?

The charge against the Protestant Reformed Churches that they are Anabaptist accuses them of fleeing the world physically, of separating themselves from the wicked society of unbelieving men and women in a physical manner. This was characteristic of certain Baptists at the time of the Reformation ("*Ana*baptists" are those religious people who practiced the re-baptism of those who were baptized in infancy). Their religious descendants and disciples today would be the Amish and the Hutterites, who try to live by themselves in their own colonies, thus separating themselves as much as possible from a wicked world in a physical way.

Kuyper called the opponents of his theory of common grace Anabaptists. Kuyper's common grace disciples today thus slander the Protestant Reformed Churches, because these churches reject Kuyper's teaching that by virtue of common grace Reformed Christians should cooperate with the ungodly in the cultural work of Christianizing the Netherlands, the United States, and the entire world. The accusation of Anabaptism is false because the rejection of common grace, and its project of Christianizing the world, does not consist of nor lead to a physical withdrawal from society or a physical separation from the wicked world.

The separation from the ungodly world that the Protestant Reformed Churches advocate and practice, more or less faithfully, is spiritual, not physical. The theological, Reformed name for this (spiritual) separation is "antithesis." Christians are *in* the world physically, while resisting being *of* the world spiritually (John 17:14–16). Christians not only may, but also are called by God to live and work in the creation of God, in all its ordinances, for example, marriage and labor. They use and enjoy all its elements, for example, education and science, right in the midst of the ungodly, at the symphony at Orchestra Hall in Chicago, or in the financial world of Wall Street, or at some factory or other. But the Christian does all and enjoys all in obedience to the law of God, out of love for God in the heart, and to God's glory. Thus the Christian separates himself from the ungodly in a spiritual manner.

The result of this spiritual separation, sometimes, is that he brings down on himself the scorn and hatred of the ungodly and is even driven out of society. As Jesus "suffered without the gate," so may it also happen to us that we are driven "without the camp, bearing his reproach" (Heb. 13:12–13).

But this is not because we voluntarily flee the "camp" after the manner of the old Anabaptists. It is due rather to the persecuting efforts of those who hate and despise the Christian life of holiness.

The charge by the Protestant Reformed Churches against the Kuyperian and Christian Reformed doctrine of common grace is that it unites Christian and non-Christian by a purported *grace* of God, thus uniting them very closely—in the *grace of God*—and illicitly. The theory of common grace also unites believers and unbelievers in a supposedly great work of God's grace in history, namely, making the world Christian. This is transgression of the antithesis. The result, as history has abundantly shown, is not that the ungodly culture of the Netherlands or of Grand Rapids has become Christian, but that the Reformed churches and people engaged in Kuyper's common grace project have become thoroughly worldly—worldly in their thinking, worldly in their behavior. Transgression of the antithesis is visited by God with the appropriate punishment of worldliness. And worldliness is spiritually fatal.

The charge against the Protestant Reformed Churches that their rejection of common grace is Anabaptist and that they are guilty of world flight is ridiculous. It is worse: it is mere name calling. No Reformed person should take the charge seriously. The lives of the members of the Protestant Reformed Churches give the lie to the charge. For myself, I regard the charge as proof positive that the opponents of the Protestant Reformed Churches are reduced to desperation in their controversy with us over common grace.

Recently I read that in 1924, when the controversy over common grace was raging in the Christian Reformed Church, Louis Berkhof, the main author of the Christian Reformed Church's three points of common grace, warned some of his Christian Reformed colleagues not to accuse Hoeksema of Anabaptism, because the charge was simply false.

I have two questions for those who perpetuate the calumny. First, is world flight the fundamental sin of, and danger for,

Reformed churches and people today? Or is the real sin and danger that they are being swallowed up by the ungodly world? How much warning against conformity to the world is given in the common grace churches by the enthusiastic proponents of common grace? Second, does a reading of the history of Israel in the Old Testament and a perusal of the admonitions of the New Testament indicate that the main threat to the church is world flight or worldliness?

Regarding my questioner's suggestion that the foes of the Protestant Reformed Churches charge against them that they are Anabaptist because these churches refuse to preach to the world that God loves all men, this may very well be partly the real cause of the false charge. After all, in its dogma of the three points of common grace, the Christian Reformed Church connected its doctrine of a common grace of God that enables godless humans to perform good works of making their culture and society Christian with the doctrine of a saving love and grace of God for all humans without exception (their well-meant offer). It stands to reason that objection to any aspect of the three points of common grace, including the denial of a saving love of God for all humans, will be branded as Anabaptist.

5. If all have common grace, why do many have no problem killing those who don't believe like them? Why do many live a depraved life until death? Do they have ability to reject common grace, according to Kuyper?

These related questions make the valid point that many humans, who are all supposed to possess the common grace of God that makes one moral, decent, and concerned for the welfare of human society, plainly show themselves desperately, indeed totally, depraved. Their thinking and behavior contradict Kuyper's theory of common grace. False religionists, for example Muslims, and multitudes of humans over all the world, all of whom are supposed to be the beneficiaries of God's common grace, either murder Christians or live grossly ungodly and immoral lives. Experience thus refutes the theory of common grace.

Add to this that Kuyper himself astoundingly acknowledged that the final result of common grace would be antichrist and his kingdom. Common grace will produce the beast of Revelation 13.[1] This explanation of common grace reduces the theory to absurdity, if not blasphemy. Grace—the grace of *God*—produces antichrist! The Protestant Reformed Churches may be excused for declining to participate in a project that produces the antichrist.

This godlessness is not due to the rejection of common grace by wicked humans, but to the working of common grace itself.

The murderous hatred of humans for other humans throughout history and the depravity that all humans share and that many openly display simply contradict Kuyper's theory of common grace. The theory of common grace is not only condemned by scripture, but also is refuted by history and experience.

6. To what do we attribute an orderly society, alleviation of poverty, judicial fairness, efforts to be sure we have clean air and clean water?

The answer given to these questions by the defenders of a common grace of God is that such desirable qualities of human life in society are the product of a common grace of God toward and in all humans without exception, ungodly as well as godly.

To this answer, before I give an answer, I have this question: "To what do we attribute all the disorder in society; the grinding poverty not only in some quarters of the United States and Canada, but also in other nations where people are starving to death daily; rampant judicial corruption not only

---

1 Kuyper, "Common Grace," in Bratt, *Abraham Kuyper: A Centennial Reader*, 179–82.

in third world countries, but also in the United States (I lived for fourteen years in Cook County in Illinois); and pollution of air and water in many parts of the world?" In addition, how does my questioner account for the devastating wars in history with their unspeakable miseries? The common grace implicit in the question to me has not been abundantly evident in history, is not abundantly evident in many countries and among many peoples today, and even in the United States and Canada is contradicted by the widespread miseries of poverty, sickness, suffering of all kinds, and painful death.

Staring every sentient human squarely in the face is the terrible wrath of God upon the entire human race outside of Jesus Christ, cursing the race, inflicting innumerable griefs and miseries, and finally ravaging the race with death, including the sorrow of bereavement. Then for many there is eternal hell. For this, common grace has no explanation. To this, common grace apparently is blind. This, common grace denies or attempts to mitigate.

"The wages of sin is death" (Rom. 6:23). "The curse of the LORD is in the house of the wicked"—the house of the healthy family of ungodly people, as well as the house of the ungodly family stricken by cancer, but obviously the house of the sick and dying (Prov. 3:33).

Rather than minimize or explain away the common curse, the advocates of common grace ought to press the truth of the common curse, in the outpouring of the wrath of God upon a guilty human race, upon the ungodly, so that they take refuge where alone refuge is to be found, namely, the particular, saving grace of God in the cross of Jesus Christ. We have this against the theory of common grace: that it weakens the urgent call of the gospel that sinners flee the wrath and curse of God by believing the gospel.

Regarding the earthly prosperity that some ungodly persons enjoy all their earthly life, Psalm 73 is the clear, awful explanation. The explanation is not that of a common grace of God. The explanation rather is that God is setting these prosperous wicked in slippery places and thus casting them down into destruction. Their earthly prosperity is worse for them than are the miserable circumstances of other ungodly persons. Their prosperity blinds and hardens them regarding their end in hell when their brief life is ended, whereas the misery of other ungodly persons may be used by God to awaken them to their plight outside of God's grace in Jesus Christ. There is no fool so foolish, and so certainly doomed, as a rich, fat, healthy fool.

Then comes along the preacher of a common grace of God to assure the prosperous ungodly and the rich fool that God in grace toward him is blessing him with prosperity and riches!

Advocates of common grace debate these issues as though they were merely academic matters. For myself, I reject the teaching of common grace in no small part because I fear to make myself responsible for the perishing of the prosperous wicked. I do not want such a man or woman to turn toward me on the great day of judgment and cry out, "Why did you not warn me? Why did you contribute to my spiritual folly and ignorance, which bring me to hell, by assuring me of God's grace toward me and of his blessing of me? Why did you not testify to me the message of Psalm 73?"

Because of the great, if not decisive, importance of the teaching of Psalm 73 regarding the controversy over an alleged common grace of God to the ungodly in their material prosperity, I may refer this questioner, and others who share his conception of the prosperity of the wicked, to my thorough exposition of the psalm in book form (*Prosperous Wicked and Plagued Saints*).

It belongs to a complete answer to the question posed here that I remind the questioner of God's providence. God's providence is his power upholding and governing the creation he made in the beginning. In his providence, God maintains even the ungodly in their humanity, so that they can develop the creation, uncovering and using its bounties; order their society, especially by government; and in general direct their life together in such a way as to benefit themselves and avoid many evils.

But providence is not inherently grace and blessing, not even in the instances in which providence provides the ungodly with many good gifts, for example order in society, or health, or nourishing food. The things themselves are good, but if God gives them to a man or woman in his wrath and if the man or woman uses and enjoys them without acknowledgment of God the giver, without gratitude to God, and without a use of them that serves God, the things are a curse to the one who so misuses them. The Heidelberg Catechism sharply distinguishes God's (good) gifts and his blessing, that is, providence and grace: "without thy blessing [grace] neither our care and labor nor thy gifts [providence] can profit us."[2]

The good things of providence mentioned in the question, namely, "an orderly society, alleviation of poverty," and the rest, are blessings to the elect believer in the grace of God to him or her in Jesus Christ, as also disorder in society, poverty, sickness, and death are blessings to him or her. To the reprobate unbeliever, all the good things of providence are a curse in divine wrath, exposing his inexcusable wickedness and increasing his guilt.

7. Could not common grace be a cultural expression of what is taught in article 36 of the Belgic Confession as it teaches on the role of a civil government to restrain evil and aid the church in the church doing her work? If God uses government in this way, why not other civic and cultural expressions also? Or do you take issue with the Belgic Confession?

As a matter of fact, I do take issue with the Belgic Confession in article 36 concerning civil government. I have stated and explained my disagreement publicly in writing. But my issue with the Belgic Confession in article 36 is not the teaching that you assume is the teaching of the article. My issue is the

---

2   Heidelberg Catechism A 125, in Schaff, *Creeds of Christendom*, 3:353.

teaching of article 36 that the civil government has the calling from God to use its sword power to promote the kingdom
of Christ and to "remove and prevent all idolatry and false
worship."[3] This I deny. The church gives me the right to take
issue with this aspect of article 36 by the footnote appended
to the article.

> This phrase, touching the office of the magistracy in its
> relation to the church, proceeds on the principle of the
> established church…History, however, does not support
> the principle of state domination over the church, but
> rather the separation of church and state. Moreover, it is
> contrary to the new dispensation that authority be vested
> in the state arbitrarily to reform the church, and to deny
> the church the right of independently conducting its own
> affairs as a distinct territory alongside the state. The New
> Testament does not subject the Christian church to the
> authority of the state, that it should be governed and
> extended by political measures, but to our Lord and King
> only, as an independent territory alongside and altogether
> independent of the state, that it may be governed and
> edified by its officebearers, and with spiritual weapons only.[4]

Your contention is entirely different. Your contention is
that article 36 of the Belgic Confession teaches a common
grace of God to all the citizens of a nation in the institution
of civil government. I call attention to the fact that the article
says nothing about civil government's being an agency of
common grace, that is, a grace bestowed upon all humans
without exception. The article speaks of "*our* gracious God,"
that is, the God of grace toward those whom the preceding
articles of the creed have described as God's elect church (see
article 16). The article itself refers to the grace of God that
is operative through civil government to the citizens of the
kingdom of Christ, that is, the members of the church.

---

3   Belgic Confession 36, in ibid., 3:432.

4   *Confessions and Church Order*, 74.

In his grace to the *church*, God has established civil government with the office, according to the article, of protecting the sacred ministry and of promoting the kingdom of Christ. This is grace to the church. According to the article, government must destroy the kingdom of antichrist by punishing the ungodly, perhaps even killing them. This is certainly not grace to the citizens of the antichristian kingdom.

The article teaches a particular, discriminating grace of God operative in and by means of civil government.

Regarding government's restraint of sin in civil society and its promotion of good order and decency, government does this by means, states the article, of "the sword," that is, earthly punishments of fines, imprisonment, and execution. This is not the same as the inner, spiritual restraint of sin in the ungodly that is the teaching of the theory of common grace. This theory, also as taught by Kuyper, teaches that God restrains sin in the unbeliever by common grace so that the unregenerated sinner is not totally depraved. Common grace enables him to do good works in the realm of civil society.

This is a denial of the doctrine of total depravity, as confessed in question 8 of the Heidelberg Catechism: "But are we *so* far depraved that we are *wholly* unapt to *any* good, and prone to *all* evil? Yes; unless we are born again by the Spirit of God."[5] This is a denial also of article 4 of the third and fourth heads of doctrine of the Canons of Dordt. With regard to the "glimmerings of natural light" that enable unbelieving humans to discover "some regard for virtue, good order in society, and for maintaining an orderly external deportment," the Canons state that the unsaved, unbelieving human is "incapable of using it [this light of nature] aright even in things natural and civil."[6]

Restraint of the deeds of violence and disorder in society by threat of punishment is essentially different from the restraining of sin in a human's heart and life by a working of (common) grace within him.

---

5   Heidelberg Catechism Q 8, in ibid., 3:310; emphasis added.

6   Canons of Dordt 3-4.4, in ibid., 3:588.

The Christian Reformed Church appealed to article 36 of the Belgic Confession in support of its doctrine of common grace, just as does this questioner. Somewhere Hoeksema responded to this appeal to article 36 with the remark that the synod of the Christian Reformed Church evidently did not know the difference between an earthly sword and the spiritual grace of God.

8. How is Kuyper's common grace related to the "two kingdoms" idea?

This question indicates a praiseworthy awareness of recent developments in the Reformed community of churches and seminaries regarding the debate over common grace. Of late, certain Reformed theologians, who present themselves as conservative, react against the development of the doctrine of common grace in their churches by its enthusiastic proponents. This development consists of calling Reformed Christians to unite with the godless in a crusade of transforming society, redeeming the culture, and Christianizing the world. The tell-tale words are "transforming," "redeeming," and "Christianizing." This crusade parades itself as the realizing of the kingdom of God in history and over all the world. Especially the Reformed high schools and colleges associated with the churches committed to the doctrine of common grace promote this grandiose scenario.

Christianizing the world is the stated purpose of the recent cooperation of Reformed theologians and the strongly Roman Catholic–influenced Acton Institute in the translation into English for the first time of Kuyper's three volumes on common grace.[7]

Realizing that this supposedly divine calling of high school and college students is erroneous, and also that it has resulted in the gross worldliness of the educational institutions and of the young people who have espoused the

---

7   See the first translated volume, *Common Grace: Noah–Adam*, especially the editors' introduction (xi–xiv) and the introduction by Richard J. Mouw (xix–xxx).

project, to say nothing of the obvious failure of the mission both in the Netherlands and in the United States over the past one hundred years, some Reformed theologians in the very churches that preach transformation, redemption, and Christianization of society and of the world by a common grace of God are challenging this notion and mission.

Instead, these critics of the notion of a Christianizing of society propose the idea of "two kingdoms." What is meant is that the Reformed Christian lives in two distinct kingdoms. He is, on the one hand, a citizen of the spiritual kingdom of Jesus Christ. As a citizen of this kingdom, he lives a life of love for God, obeying the commandments of the law of God. Especially on the Lord's day, he worships God in and with the church. But on the other hand, he is also a citizen of some earthly nation. As a citizen of this earthly nation, he simply lives the earthly life of this nation, obeying its laws and conducting himself pretty much as do the unbelieving citizens of the nation. In contrast to his life as a citizen of the kingdom of Christ, which is "other-worldly," his life as a citizen of the United States or Canada is "this-worldly."[8]

One can rejoice that Reformed theologians finally take note of the devastating effects of the doctrine of common grace in their churches, especially on the high school and college students, although one would have to be blind not to see them. But these Reformed theologians refuse to recognize and acknowledge that the source of the evils is the doctrine of a common grace of God that is supposed to have these Christianizing effects and this divine, world-transforming purpose. Indeed, these theologians themselves vigorously defend the doctrine of common grace that is the cause of the evils to which they are opposed. They are as bitter enemies of the Protestant Reformed rejection of common grace as are

---

8 For a defense of this conception of the Reformed, Christian life, see David Van Drunen, *Living in God's Two Kingdoms: A Biblical Vision for Christianity and Culture* (Crossway, 2010). For a fuller critique of the book and its doctrine of the Christian life in two kingdoms, see my review of Van Drunen's book in the November 2014 issue of the *Protestant Reformed Theological Journal* (48 no. 1, 118–25).

the traditional, Christian Reformed proponents of common grace. As long as they defend Kuyper's theory of cultural common grace, their opposition to the implications and effects of the theory is an exercise in futility. The only way to destroy an evil in the church, as in nature, is to uproot it.

In addition, the two kingdoms conception of the Christian life is seriously in error. Although the Christian lives his life in two distinct spheres or kingdoms—the earthly and the heavenly—it is not true that he lives in these two kingdoms in two distinct and different ways. Much less is it true that the Christian lives life in the heavenly kingdom by particular grace but life in the earthly kingdom by common grace, which he shares with the ungodly. To propose this is the repudiation of the very essence of the Reformed, Christian life. The Christian lives his one life in one manner and by one grace of God: as a citizen of the kingdom of Jesus Christ by particular, saving grace. As such a citizen, he lives on the Lord's day in worship in a true church and on the other days in his spiritual devotions of prayer and reading and study of the Bible by the particular, sanctifying grace of God in Jesus Christ.

Also as such a citizen, by particular, sanctifying grace he lives all his life, throughout the week, in marriage and the family, on the job, either ruling or submitting in the sphere of government, in his relationships with the neighbor, at play, and in every other aspect of his earthly life in this world. He lives a full earthly life, in all the ordinances and spheres of creation, and he lives this earthly life by the power of the one, saving, particular grace of God and in accordance with the law of God.

By living so, he very evidently shows himself to be spiritually separated from the ungodly and from the ungodly nature of their use (misuse, really) of God's creation and its ordinances. This is the antithesis—a fundamental description of the Christian life in the world by the Reformed faith on the basis of the Bible, and the description that the doctrine of common grace obliterates.

Inasmuch as the two kingdoms theology refuses to repudiate common grace and fails to proclaim the antithesis established by the one, particular, saving grace of God in Jesus Christ by the Holy Spirit, the two kingdoms theology is and must be a failure.

9. To what extent (if at all) did Abraham Kuyper make the Reformed confessions the basis of the Free University?

Undoubtedly, there is more to this question than meets the eye.

The simple answer to the question is that Kuyper refused to make the Reformed confessions the basis of the Free University that he founded. Since the Free University included the theological, seminary training of prospective pastors in the Reformed Churches in the Netherlands, the Reformed confessions were not, and are not, the basis even of the theological instruction.

Kuyper saw to it that the official basis of the Free University was rather "Reformed Principles." Kuyper's own justification of this ground of his university was to avoid bringing the instruction under the authority of the church. It was an expression of his idea of "sphere sovereignty." This phrase was, in fact, the title of Kuyper's inaugural address on the opening of the university on October 20, 1880: *Souvereiniteit in Eigen Kring* (Sphere sovereignty).[9]

As the first and chief of these Reformed principles, Kuyper himself in his inaugural address mentioned the sovereignty of God. Kuyper's intention was that the sovereignty of God be honored in all departments of the university.

Regardless of Kuyper's intentions, it should have been obvious to everyone, including Kuyper, that it is grievous error to fail to make the Reformed confessions explicitly the basis of the theological instruction of men for the Reformed ministry.

---

9   For the English translation of the bulk of Kuyper's address, see Bratt, *Abraham Kuyper: A Centennial Reader*, 461–90; regarding the founding of the university explicitly "on the basis of Reformed Principles," see Heslam, *Creating a Christian Worldview*, 46–48.

In addition, it is a mistake to regard the Reformed creeds as an ecclesiastical intrusion upon and illicit narrowing of the studies in the other faculties of a Reformed university. As the true summary of the content of holy scripture, the Reformed creeds are the foundation of all the life of Reformed Christians, including their educational life and labor. They are not narrowly ecclesiastical. They do not illicitly restrict and hamper the scientific study at a university or, for that matter, at a grade school. The creeds, like the Bible of which they are the accurate summary, rather ground Christian study and learning, circumscribe the lawful, truthful endeavor of education, and guard against false and pernicious theories.

One might as well object to having the Bible as the basis of the school as object to the Reformed creeds. In fact, objection to the creeds *is* objection to the teaching of the Bible.

One may justifiably suspect that Kuyper's rejection of the Reformed confessions as the basis of his university in favor of the general "Reformed Principles" was motivated by his attraction to common grace and its influence upon the studies at the university. For Kuyper, common grace and its supposed influence upon Christian cultural, particularly academic, pursuits moved him in the direction of "Reformed Principles," common grace being an important such principle, rather than in the direction of the Reformed confessions, from which common grace is notably missing. No doubt, Kuyper argued that basing a Reformed university upon the creeds would have been a serious narrowing of the educational enterprise.

Regardless of Kuyper's thinking, history has made abundantly plain that the exclusion of the creeds from the basis of the university and the general reference instead to principles have contributed to the gross apostasy of that once Reformed school. Today, the theological department of the Free University is a school of false prophets. The instruction in the other departments differs little from the antichristian instruction in the state universities. The Free University did not oppose the recent union of Kuyper's denomination of churches, the Reformed Churches in the Netherlands, with the apostate state church and a liberal Lutheran church in forming the un-Reformed and apostate Protestant Church in the Netherlands (PKN). The university supported and went along with this ecumenicity, an ecumenicity in which the Reformed confessions were not only not determinative, but also abandoned.

The Reformed confessions determine and safeguard genuinely "Reformed Principles," including the determination that common grace is an un- and anti-Reformed principle.

10. You charge in the speech that the United Reformed Churches are now busy in the development of common grace. Where do you see this being written and happening?

The reference to the United Reformed Churches in the speech—the only mention of the United Reformed Churches in the lecture—to which this question alludes was the following: "[In view of the destructive influence of common grace on Kuyper's churches and university and on the Christian Reformed Church and its college—Calvin College], why do the United Reformed Churches, which recently split from the Christian Reformed Church exactly over the disastrous, world-conforming effects of common grace, particularly the world's thinking about the relation of men and women with regard to women in church office—why do the United Reformed Churches refuse to acknowledge the root of the evil but instead themselves contend for common grace as vigorously as the Christian Reformed Church and now cooperate in spreading the destructive doctrine of common grace?" The beginning of the next paragraph in the lecture was, "The Kuyperian theory of common grace with the practice that accompanies it is ecclesiastical suicide!"

Proof of the implied charge in this question about the United Reformed Churches is, first, simply that the United Reformed Churches have not explicitly and vehemently repudiated the false doctrine of common grace, even though that doctrine was in fact the cause of the evil in the Christian Reformed Church against which the United Reformed Churches objected and largely because of which the United Reformed Churches split the Christian Reformed Church, namely, the evil of women in ecclesiastical office. This silence is telling. The United Reformed Churches rejected the fruit of the doctrine of common grace but deliberately and persistently preserve the root.

James D. Bratt, himself certainly no critic of the theory of common grace, observes that already in Kuyper's day "conservative critics...saw in common grace a license for world conformity."[10]

All the more culpable are the United Reformed Churches in refusing to repudiate the theory of common grace in view of the analysis of Kuyper's doctrine by some of the most liberal Dutch Reformed theologians. Hendrikus Berkhof is representative. Berkhof explains the doctrine of common grace of Kuyper and Bavinck as their answer to the main issue that has mesmerized Christian theology in Europe for the past two hundred years: how to relate Christian theology positively to the thinking of the non-Christian world, that is, how to relate the church and the world, how to relate the church and the world *positively.*

According to Berkhof, the fundamental issue in contemporary theology is the "relationship between the gospel and the secularized culture of [the] day." In the past two hundred years, a leading concern, if not the main concern, of European theologians has been the "attempt to bring about a reconciliation between the gospel and the spirit of modernity." In other words, theologians "tried more or less deliberately to build a bridge between the gospel and their secularized cultural environment."[11]

Kuyper and Bavinck shared this concern and exerted themselves in this effort, Bavinck, if anything, more vigorously

---

10 Bratt, ed., "Common Grace," in Bratt, *Abraham Kuyper: A Centennial Reader,* 166.

11 Berkhof, *Two Hundred Years of Theology,* 65, 131, xiii.

than Kuyper. The doctrine by which Kuyper and Bavinck attempted to bridge the divide between gospel and church, on the one hand, and the "spirit of modernity," that is, the world, on the other hand, was common grace.[12] In the context of his analysis of Kuyper's attempt to bridge the divide between the gospel and ungodly culture, between the church and the world, by his doctrine of common grace, Berkhof judges Kuyper's doctrine of common grace to be un-Reformed: "In theology—*apart from his broad development of the doctrine of common grace*—Kuyper closely followed the Calvinistic tradition."[13]

I observe that prominent theologians and ministers in the Christian Reformed Church in North America in the early twentieth century, including Ralph Janssen, Johannes Groen, and many others, enthusiastically shared this conviction that the calling of Reformed theology was to bridge the gospel and the culture, and they zealously pursued this goal. This explains the antipathy in the Christian Reformed Church to Danhof and Hoeksema, the distaste for the truth and practice of the antithesis, the readiness ecclesiastically to destroy ministers recognized by all, including the synod that condemned them, as orthodox Reformed men, and the determination to adopt the three points of common grace. Common grace was to be the bridge from the church to the world—and proved to be the bridge from the world into the church!

What this means is that in opposing the theory of common grace in the early 1920s, Hoeksema was up against far more than a few theologians, a synod of Reformed churches, or even the entire denomination of the Christian Reformed Church. He was opposing the gigantic, massive "spirit of the age," which was and is the spirit of antichrist, which is in reality Satan. That spirit had as its purpose the destruction in the Christian Reformed Church of the antithesis—the spiritual separation and uncompromising warfare between

12   Ibid., 108-14.

13   Ibid., 109; emphasis added.

the church and the world of the ungodly ("enmity," in the language of Genesis 3:15)—and the adoption and practice by the Christian Reformed Church of conformity to this world. Having come to know Hoeksema as I have, I have no doubt that he was fully aware that this, and nothing less, was the nature of his controversy in the Christian Reformed Church over Kuyperian, and then in addition Arminian, common grace. (Common grace is Arminian in that the decisions of the 1924 synod of the Christian Reformed Church adopted the heresy of the well-meant offer of the gospel—a universal, saving love of God for all humans that is ineffectual to save many.)

The "spirit of the age" crushed and killed Hoeksema ecclesiastically in the early 1920s, as he must have known it would. But it did not, and could not, snuff out his witness to particular grace and the antithesis. This is the witness of the risen, almighty Jesus Christ himself. Nothing and no one can snuff out this witness—not antichrist, not Satan himself.

This witness continues in the Protestant Reformed Churches. If these churches silence this witness or even weaken it, probably because of misguided zeal for ecumenicity, God will raise up another church to bear witness to the truth. If need be, he will cause the stones to cry out, "Come out from among them, and be ye separate, saith the Lord... and I will receive you, and will be a Father unto you, and ye shall be my sons and daughters, saith the Lord Almighty" (2 Cor. 6:17–18).

What the most liberal scholars clearly see and frankly acknowledge concerning Kuyper's cultural common grace, the confessionally conservative United Reformed Churches are unable to recognize, even though this common grace has ruined the church from which they have separated themselves. If they do recognize the ruinous effects of common grace upon the antithesis and upon the church, they lack the grace and courage to condemn the false doctrine and eradicate it from their theology and federation of churches.

Second, the leading theologians in the United Reformed Churches and in the seminaries that train the ministers of the

United Reformed Churches freely and repeatedly throughout their writings, whether in *Christian Renewal* or in books, commend the doctrine of common grace as their own theological conviction and defend the doctrine against the attack on it by the Protestant Reformed Churches (although they usually are careful not to mention these churches or explicitly to indicate that the questioning of common grace against which they are defending rises from these churches). If there is one minister in the United Reformed Churches who rejects the three points of common grace as adopted by the Christian Reformed Church in 1924, or who rejects Kuyper's doctrine of cultural common grace, I would be surprised, indeed astounded. If there is one, he has not made his opposition to common grace known.

I do know that many of the men who plotted and then executed the schism in the Christian Reformed Church that resulted in the formation of the United Reformed Churches saw the Christian Reformed Church's doctrine of common grace as contributing significantly to the apostasy of the Christian Reformed Church, on account of which they felt themselves called to split the church. In the words of one of them at an informal meeting of several, to which I had been invited and at which I was present, in South Holland, Illinois, "The doctrine of common grace has done nothing but damage to the Christian Reformed Church since its adoption."

So entrenched in the theology of the seminary professors presently training many of the seminarians of the United Reformed Churches is the doctrine of a common grace of God that they do not argue on behalf of it but assume it. This is evident in the writings of most, if not all, of the professors at Mid-America Reformed Seminary in the Chicago area and at Westminster West Seminary in southern California. Typical is the line of David Van Drunen, professor of theology at Westminster West, one of the main seminaries used by the men of the United Reformed Churches. In a book that expressly treats the relation of the Reformed Christian and worldly culture, Van Drunen asserts that "unbelievers...live in this world...under God's providential common grace." This in passing, as one might observe that the sun rose this morning in the east. Nevertheless, it is this common grace that "obligates" believers "to cooperate as much as possible with unbelieving practitioners of their discipline."

From this common grace blessing by God of the scholarly work of unbelievers, Van Drunen draws the weighty implication that Christian schools are not necessary. Whether to establish and use Christian schools or to use the state schools, where from the instruction is banned the Bible, prayer, and the confession of the one, triune God, the creator and governor of the universe and all its aspects—ultimate and foundational reality—to say nothing of the banning of the truth that Jesus Christ is the "firstborn of every creature" (Col. 1:15), is merely "a matter of Christian liberty."[14]

Common grace is the death of the good Christian school. Common grace consigns the lambs of Jesus Christ to the tender mercies of the wolves ravening at the antichristian state schools. So much for the covenant of God in Jesus Christ with the children of believers! This ought to be of some concern to Reformed parents in the United Reformed Churches, as in the Christian Reformed Church, who treasure the covenant of God with their baptized children and who love their children and grandchildren for God's sake.

Third, when I mentioned the United Reformed Churches in the lecture, I had very much in mind the acknowledgment in the first volume of the translation of Kuyper's three volumes on common grace that among the institutions providing "financial support and leadership" for the project of making Kuyper's work available in English, and thus promoting the project of Christianizing America, is "Mid-America Reformed Seminary."[15] Mid-America is perhaps the main seminary supported and used by the United Reformed Churches for the training of their ministers. Thus the United

---

14 Van Drunen, *Living in God's Two Kingdoms*, 181, 183.

15 Kuyper, *Common Grace: Noah-Adam*, xv.

Reformed Churches are publicly and vigorously promoting the theory of common grace and its implementation in North America in 2016.

11. How do Reformed theologians who adhere to common grace attempt to maintain orthodox eschatology when the goals of common grace appear to lead toward [Christian] Reconstruction and millennialist theology instead of amillennialism?

Kuyper's theory of common grace lends itself to, and is used today on behalf of, the doctrine of the last things known as postmillennialism. Very simply, this is the theory of the last things that holds that Christians will, and are called by God to, influence culture, first in their own nation and then in all the world. Thus the world becomes Christian, if not by the conversion of all humans, then by the dominating influence of Christianity upon all aspects of culture—government, media, education, the arts, and more.

This will last for a thousand years ("millennium") or, according to some postmillennial enthusiasts, especially the Christian Reconstructionists, hundreds of thousands of years. Jesus, unfortunately excluded from this earthly triumph of his kingdom, being out of sight, tucked away in heaven while his postmillennial agents rule the world, will then come back to earth to inaugurate the everlasting kingdom of God in the new creation, at which time his kingdom ends. (In one of the oddest twists in all the history of kingdoms, Jesus the king will be absent from his kingdom during all the time of its supremacy on earth. This is not a problem for the postmillennialists, particularly the Reconstructionists, whom you mention, because they have designs on the throne themselves.)

Postmillennialism preaches an earthly, worldwide victory of the kingdom of Christ *within* history, prior to the end. Necessarily, therefore, they preach a carnal kingdom.

The theory of common grace promotes this postmillennial hope of the church. The very language of the theory indicates its postmillennial implication. Christians cooperating with unbelievers *transform*, *redeem*, and *Christianize* society and the world. Since this world-transforming, redeeming, and Christianizing movement takes place by common grace, common grace is the power that will achieve the postmillennial dream. Even though some of the enthusiastic proponents of common grace tend to underplay, if not ignore altogether, the postmillennial nature of their theory (well aware that their church and creeds are amillennial), the theology and language of common grace are definitely postmillennial.

This is still one more proof of the un-Reformed nature of common grace, for Reformed theology is confessionally amillennial.

One thing is undeniably evident in the enthusiastic advocacy of common grace and its prospects in history by its most fervent promoters, for example, Richard J. Mouw in his introduction to the first volume of the translation of Kuyper's *Common Grace* into English. Evident is that not much is made of the antithesis, the separation and warfare between the children of the devil and the children of God. The emphasis, if not the whole of the view of history especially in these last days, is "God's marvelous designs for human cultural life," although to give credit where credit is due, Mouw does note, indeed warn, along the way of his promotion of the postmillennial implications of common grace that the antithesis is a "dreadful reality."[16] How the antithesis comports with common grace, Mouw does not inform us.

Disconcerting for the advocates of a lovely, postmillennial, earthly kingdom of Christ in history as the outcome of the common grace program of God is Kuyper's own doctrine that the force and outcome of the common grace adventure of Christians and unbelievers united will be the kingdom not of Christ but of antichrist. Common grace will produce the beast of Revelation 13: "The closing scene in the drama of

---

16 Richard J. Mouw, "Introduction," in Kuyper, *Common Grace: Noah–Adam,* xxx.

common grace can be enacted only through the appearance on stage of the man of sin."[17] More emphatically still: "The appearing of the 'man of sin' will be brought about exactly by the operation of common grace."[18]

Let the disciples of the Kuyper of common grace take heed! According to their master himself, they unite closely with the wicked world in a great work of a grace of God within and upon mankind. Thus they open up themselves, their children, and their institutions to the deleterious effects of the influence on them of the ungodly world. In addition, they cooperate, in this common grace venture, in bringing forth the antichrist and his beastly kingdom. For doing so, they will be held responsible by God. Knowing that they are doing so makes them fully responsible for their common grace activity.

Let the Reformed world take note also of this: the Protestant Reformed Churches are determined neither to bridge the chasm between the world and the church, so that the world can influence their members, nor to pave the way for the coming of antichrist. If these determinations are reprehensible, let someone say so, and demonstrate it.

Even though Kuyper was amillennial in his doctrine of the last things, despite the postmillennial implications of his theory of common grace, his theory of common grace did influence him to propose an erroneous, even odd, aspect of eschatology. Kuyper thought that the products of common grace would gain entrance into the new world, so as to enhance the beauty and splendor of the new heavens and the new earth. Such was his commitment to common grace that at least in its effects common grace would continue into and adorn eternity. Eternity will everlastingly expose and distress Herman Hoeksema and the Protestant Reformed Churches!

With appeal to Revelation 21:26, "They shall bring the

---

17 See the full, frank statement of this eschatology in "Common Grace," in Bratt, *Abraham Kuyper: A Centennial Reader*, 179–82.

18 Kuyper, *De Gemeene Gratie*, 1:443; the translation of the Dutch is mine. This part of volume 1 has not yet appeared in English translation.

glory and honour of the nations into it [the holy city in the new creation]," Kuyper wrote that the "fruit of common grace" in the cultural accomplishments of the nations (he mentions England and Germany) will not "simply perish and be annihilated in the universal destruction of the world by fire [at the end], but this fruit will have significance for the new Jerusalem, that is, for the new earth." In new manifestations, "all the forms in which now the fruit of common grace flourishes...do not perish, but remain, then to be brought into the new kingdom of glory."[19] In some new form, Beethoven's symphonies, Rembrandt's paintings, and Dickens's novels, as well, very likely, as Balanchine's dances and Spielberg's movies, will have a place in and embellish the new creation, according to Kuyper's theory of common grace.

Kuyper is mistaken in every respect. The cultural achievements of the great, ungodly musicians, artists, and writers are the expression not of common grace but of the great abilities of humans, who were originally made in the image of God and who still, by God's preserving providence, display their abilities as humans and, though fallen, retain some of their natural gifts.

Second, the glory and honor of the nations that will be brought into the new world, according to Revelation 21:26, are not the artistic works of the ungodly. All of those works will perish in the "fervent heat" that will destroy the present creation and its works at the end (2 Pet. 3:10). With reference to the prophecy of Isaiah 60, that the Gentiles ("nations," in Rev. 21:26) shall come to the light of Zion, Revelation 21 foretells that in the elect among them the Gentile nations will share in the salvation of the "new Jerusalem, coming down from God out of heaven" at the very end of history (v. 2).

The glory and the honor of the nations of Revelation 21:26 are not the cultural achievements of political England and Germany or even of the Netherlands in its golden age. They are the splendor of "the nations of them which are saved"

---

19 Ibid., 1:460–61; the translation of the Dutch is mine.

(Rev. 21:24). The nations consist of the elect, believing, "saved" citizens in every nation. Their glory and honor are not cultural and carnal but holiness and spirituality—the effects in them not of a common grace of God but of his one, particular, saving grace in Jesus Christ by the Holy Ghost. Their glory is not that they wrote salacious novels, secular plays, and symphonies devoted to the glory of man, nor that they arranged seductive dances. None of these is glory. All is shame. Whatever is not done to the glory of God, whatever leaves God out, whatever has as its purpose the glory of man, is shameful, despicably shameful. The only works that are good, and thus honorable, are those done "for his [God's] glory."[20]

The glory of the nations, their *true* glory, is their worship of the one, true God; their confession of Jesus as Lord; and their life of holiness.

Common grace will no more have a place in the new world than it has in this. The new world will everlastingly validate the rejection of common grace by the Protestant Reformed Churches.

(By this answer, I have responded also to another, related question: "How is common grace connected to postmillennial theology?")

12. Will Prof. Engelsma post his list of references from the lecture to the website for this event?

Here follows the list of references, mainly to Kuyper's writings, in the lecture.

Kuyper's explanation of what he meant by "Christianizing" is found in James D. Bratt, ed., *Abraham Kuyper: A Centennial Reader* (Eerdmans, 1998), 199.

The quotation of President Le Roy of Calvin College about transforming this broken world is found in his August 2014 brochure to graduates of the college, "This Square Inch."

Kuyper distinguishes two kinds of grace with different names in Dutch in the first part of the first volume of the translation into English of his *Common Grace: Common*

---

20 Heidelberg Catechism Q&A 91, in Schaff, *Creeds of Christendom*, 3:339–40.

Grace: Noah—Adam (Grand Rapids, MI: Christian's Library Press [Acton Institute], 2013), 7–14. See also the appendix in this volume, pp. 239–41.

Kuyper's statement as to what common grace does in culture is from his *Calvinism* in the chapter on "Calvinism and Science" ([Eerdmans, 1943], 125).

The quotation of Richard Mouw is from his introduction to the first volume of the translation of Kuyper's work on common grace, listed above.

Kuyper's significant description of common grace as a "point of contact" for the gospel is in volume 1 of his three-volume work on common grace. This part of the work has not yet been translated. The translation is mine. The Dutch word used by Kuyper is *"aanrakingspunt."*[21] The entire section in which occurs the assertion that common grace is a "point of contact" for the gospel is fatal compromise of salvation by sovereign grace. Here Kuyper forgot, or compromised, what he had written earlier in defense of salvation by particular, sovereign grace, in his book *Dat De Genade Particulier Is* (That grace is particular).

The Reformed confession is that there remains no point of contact for the gospel in the unregenerated sinner. A point of contact is some receptivity to the gospel in the sinner. The Reformed doctrine of total depravity rejects and condemns as heretical the teaching of a point of contact (see the Canons of Dordt, 3–4). The fallen sinner is spiritually *dead*. Just as there is no point of contact in a physically dead person for a word and work of physical resurrection, so also is there no point of contact in the spiritually dead sinner for Christ's work of spiritual resurrection. The Reformed rejection of the Pelagian and Arminian doctrine of free will, that is, a will in the unsaved sinner that is able to respond positively to the call of the gospel, is the rejection of a point of contact. The Reformed doctrine of total depravity, in Canons 3–4, is the rejection of the false doctrine of a point of contact for the gospel in natural, sinful humans.

21 Kuyper, *De Gemeene Gratie*, 1:426.

The doctrine of a common grace of God, in whatever form it appears in Reformed circles, always proves to be the corruption of the Reformed faith, especially its teaching of salvation by sovereign grace alone, by the introduction of a point of contact for the gospel.

That Kuyper began his treatment of common grace with the covenant with Noah, and what Kuyper's explanation of the Noahic covenant is, are found in the first translated volume of his work on common grace, listed above.

For Kuyper's teaching that common grace will produce the antichrist, see Bratt, *Abraham Kuyper: A Centennial Reader*, 179–82.

Kuyper charged Anabaptism against his opponents already in the foreword to his first volume on common grace. See the translation, *Common Grace: Noah–Adam*, 3–6, and often throughout the book.

Kuyper's famed statement about "not a square inch" can be found in Bratt, *Abraham Kuyper: A Centennial Reader*, 461.

13. How would Kuyper and his disciples explain Genesis 6:8, "But Noah found grace in the eyes of the Lord," and the contrast in the previous verses to judgments on the ungodly?

If Kuyper commented on Genesis 6:8, I have not come across his explanation. The text is not listed in the "text-register" at the end of volume 3 of Kuyper's three volumes on common grace. In light of his extended explanation of the history of God's gracious dealings with humankind between Adam and the flood, I suggest the following as Kuyper's explanation, attributing to him the most favorable explanation possible.

From Adam's fall to the flood, two kinds of grace of God were bestowed on members of the human race: a common grace giving earthly life and benefits, as well as restraining sin to some extent, which was enjoyed by all humans without exception; and a particular, saving grace that was given only to God's elect, including Noah. The grace that Noah found in the eyes of the Lord, according to Genesis 6:8, was the particular, saving grace of God in Jesus Christ, delivering him from the punishment and ruling power of sin and bestowing upon him eternal life, which was typified by the deliverance in the ark. This gracious attitude of the Lord toward Noah, preserving him from the wickedness of the rest of the human race, as described in verse 5, and delivering Noah by the flood, was particular; it did not rest on those who perished in the flood. This is the most favorable understanding of Kuyper's explanation of the text.

One could not be faulted, however, for concluding from Kuyper's treatment of Noah and the flood that Genesis 6:8 teaches that in the case of Noah the common grace he shared with all humans worked effectively in him so that sin was more restrained in him than in the others and that, accordingly, this common grace of God spared him from the physical destruction of drowning in the flood. According to this understanding of Kuyper, the grace of Genesis 6:8 had nothing to do with Noah's spiritual salvation but only accomplished his physical preservation.

This understanding of Kuyper is justified by the fact, which Kuyper asserted repeatedly and emphasized strongly, that Kuyper regarded the salvation of Noah and his family in the ark as merely a physical deliverance or preservation from the waters of the flood. There was nothing spiritual about Noah's deliverance in the ark. The grace of God for Noah in the flood was strictly and exclusively *"common grace."*[22]

This total misunderstanding of the salvation of Noah and his family in the ark, in the interests of Kuyper's theory of common grace, forced the Dutch theologian to corrupt all the New Testament references to Noah's salvation in the ark, including Hebrews 11:7, 1 Peter 3:20–21, and 2 Peter 2:5. All of these passages speak of the salvation of Noah and his house in the ark. Viewing Noah's salvation as merely God's physical preservation of Noah, and in him the race, by a

---

22 Kuyper, *De Gemeene Gratie*, 1:284; emphasis is Kuyper's. See also pp. 285-86.

common grace, Kuyper was compelled to explain all these New Testament passages as referring merely to physical preservation, since common grace is able to "save" only in this physical manner. Typical, and indicative at the same time of the gross twisting of the passages in the interests of his novel theory of common grace, is Kuyper's explanation of 1 Peter 3.

First Peter 3:20–21 is an especially difficult challenge to Kuyper's common grace conception of the salvation of Noah in the ark since the passage expressly makes the waters of the flood an Old Testament type ("figure") of baptism. Every Christian knows that baptism is a sign and seal not of some physical preservation but of spiritual salvation in Jesus Christ. In addition, the passage in 1 Peter expressly states that baptism, of which the flood was a type, "save[s] us ([as]...the answer of a good conscience toward God,) by the resurrection of Jesus Christ." This is spiritual salvation! Of this, the salvation of the eight souls of Noah's family by water was a type. Corresponding to New Testament baptism, the Old Testament salvation of Noah in the ark was, as to its main idea, a spiritual salvation. It was accomplished by the particular, saving grace of God in Jesus Christ.

Undeterred by the clear language of the apostle, Kuyper explained that, just as the salvation of New Testament baptism preserves elect believers from spiritual evils, so the salvation of Noah and his family was (merely) God's preservation of them physically from the destroying waters of the flood. The grace that thus preserved Noah was God's common grace. "The 'grace' displayed in the flood was not *special* grace but *common* grace. The ark did not save unto eternal life but for temporal life on earth."[23]

This explanation of the saving of Noah and his family in the ark enables Kuyper to extend the grace of this salvation to every human without exception to the end of history. All humans are the beneficiaries of a grace that spares them

---

23 Kuyper, *Common Grace: Noah–Adam*, 110; see also Kuyper, *De Gemeene Gratie*, 1:284–91.

from another flood and grants them physical life with its good things.

But Kuyper's explanation of the salvation of Noah and of the grace that accomplished this salvation is exposed as erroneous by the apostle's comparison of this salvation with that signified and accomplished by baptism, in 1 Peter 3. The salvation of baptism is spiritual and is accomplished by particular, saving grace. All humans do not share in the grace and salvation of baptism, but only the elect.

Fatal also to Kuyper's explanation of the salvation of Noah and his family is Kuyper's view that the salvation of Noah was God's saving of him *from* the waters of the flood. According to Kuyper, just as God saved Noah from the watery destruction of the flood, so he saves all humans from another worldwide flood or from some other physical destruction of the race. But the Bible does not teach that God saved Noah *from* the waters of the flood. On the contrary, God saved Noah *by means of* the waters of the flood. Such is the plain teaching of 1 Peter 3:20: "eight souls were saved *by* water."

The water of the flood was not the threat from which Noah was saved. The water of the flood was the means of Noah's salvation. The evil from which the water saved Noah and his family was the world of wicked men and women and the abounding wickedness of that world. So also baptism, as a means of grace to elect believers and their children, saves us by separating us from the world of the ungodly, washing away our own sins and sinfulness, and bringing us spiritually into the new world of covenantal communion with God. The water of baptism is not the element from which the baptized is saved but the God-ordained means of salvation from sin, including the corrupt world of fallen mankind among whom we live.

Baptism does not establish a common salvation or preservation of holy believers and unholy unbelievers. Baptism establishes the antithesis between the two groups. The same water that saves the elect destroys the reprobate unbeliever. The grace of God in Jesus Christ that justifies and sanctifies the elect believer is the judgment of the reprobate unbeliever. The cross that redeems the elect is also the judgment of the world of the ungodly (John 12:31–32).

Kuyper's common grace view of the "preservation" (Kuyper's preferred term for the salvation of Noah in the ark) of Noah fails to reckon with the biblical teaching that Noah was saved *by* the flood. This truth, in fact, exposes Kuyper's entire interpretation of Noah and the flood as utterly false. On Kuyper's own admission, his entire theory of common grace rested on his theology of Noah.

Long as this answer to the question has become (and the length is both necessary and useful in the debate over common grace, since according to the father of cultural common grace himself, the history of Noah and the flood is fundamental to the theory of common grace), this question at least allows for, if it does not demand, an additional, brief account of Kuyper's explanation of the covenant with Noah found in Genesis 9. If Kuyper's explanation of the history of Noah and of his salvation in the ark is the foundation of Kuyper's theory of cultural common grace, Kuyper's explanation of the covenant with Noah in Genesis 9 is the cornerstone of the foundation.

According to Kuyper, God's covenant with Noah after the flood, as recorded in Genesis 9, was a new and different covenant from that established with the elect human race in Genesis 3:15. It was essentially different from the covenant that would be established with Abraham in Genesis 12 and the following chapters. It was essentially different from the covenant confirmed in the cross of Christ.

The covenant with Noah was strictly and exclusively a "covenant of common grace." God established this covenant with every human without exception who would be born from Noah's three sons. This covenant had nothing to do whatever with spiritual salvation. It was purely earthly and material. It consisted only of the gift of physical life; of material benefits, for example, health, food, riches, and especially the guarantee that there would not again be a worldwide flood or similar physical destruction of the race; of a restraint of sin by an inner working of common grace in the hearts of unregenerate men and women; of a capability of these unbelievers to do much good in the sphere of natural, earthly life; and of the ability to produce gloriously good works of culture.

In this Noahic covenant there is after all nothing that intentionally or primarily pertains to *saving* grace.[24]

That *content* of the Noahic covenant lies entirely within the sphere of *natural* life, envisions *temporal* and not *eternal* goods, and applies to unbelievers just as much as it does to those who fear God...The content of this covenant is simply and plainly this: *that until the end of the world, the surface of our globe will not again be in a position to be disturbed, but will remain as it is now.*[25]

The "grace" displayed in the flood was not *special* grace but *common* grace. The ark did not save unto eternal life but for temporal life on earth...The grace shown here is not particular, restricted to the elect and leading to eternal life, but *common*.[26]

The blessing of the new situation [brought about by the flood] was intended not only for God's church, but for *everything that is human*...The grace shown here extends to the entirety of human life...Its purpose was also so that in a proper sense God the Lord would continue his work in that broad sphere of human life [culture].[27]

[The covenant with Noah] revealed an act of *general grace* or of *common grace* that is all encompassing, governing all of history, decisive for our situation, and extending into the farthest future. This common grace must be

---

24 Kuyper, *Common Grace: Noah-Adam*, 18; emphasis is Kuyper's.

25 Ibid., 33; emphasis is Kuyper's.

26 Ibid., 110; emphasis is Kuyper's.

27 Ibid., 113–14; emphasis is Kuyper's.

gratefully accepted. Our confession must take account of common grace, and our perspective of life and of the entire situation of the world must be formed on the basis of common grace.[28]

Whoever ignores or underestimates this powerful act of God's grace, and thereby also his *common grace*, distorts his view on life, ends up with a false dualism, and easily runs the risk of allowing his Christian religion to deviate from the *Reformed* track, that is, from the correct track.[29]

Evident in these representative quotations of Kuyper is not only his conception of the covenant with Noah, but also the great importance to him of this theory of common grace and its supposed embodiment in the covenant with Noah of Genesis 9. Common grace forms his worldview and determines the Reformed, Christian faith and life. Rejection of the theory of common grace is not a minor, tolerable matter to Kuyper, as it is not today to his disciples. Dissent from the theory of common grace must be punished, as the Protestant Reformed Churches can testify from painful experience. On the other hand, if Kuyper's interpretation of the covenant with Noah as a covenant of common grace is mistaken, the damage done to churches and people that have wrongly espoused and practiced it will be considerable.

The cultural aspect of the covenant of common grace was especially dear to Kuyper's heart, as it continues to be precious to Kuyper's modern disciples. They cannot let go of Kuyper's theory of common grace because of the love of their hearts for Socrates and his philosophy; for Mozart and his music; for Michelangelo and his statuary; for Raphael and his paintings; for Shakespeare and his plays. It is not enough for them that these great artists and their grand works of art be attributed to the glimmerings still in fallen man of natural light, in view of God's creation of man in his own image.

---

28 Ibid., 116–17; emphasis is Kuyper's.

29 Ibid., 116–17; emphasis is Kuyper's.

They must be honored as possessing and displaying a grace of God.

How this common grace has the hearts of these Reformed men and women is evident from the fact that, whereas they sit loose to the undermining of the confession of God's particular, saving grace, any attack on God's common grace is met with scorn, ostracism, rage, and ecclesiastical censure. You may demolish the holy synod of Dordt with impunity, but do not touch the pagan, pederast Socrates!

Since I have refuted this explanation of the covenant with Noah in the speech itself, I can be brief here. As John 3:16 and Romans 8:19–22 demonstrate, the covenant with Noah of Genesis 9 was a manifestation of the full extent of the salvation of the covenant of grace in Jesus Christ. The covenant in Jesus, established and realized by particular, saving grace, extends not only to the elect out of all nations and peoples (which is the salvation of those nations and peoples), but also to the animals and to the earth itself. It is the covenant with creation, as eternally conceived by God in Jesus Christ (Col. 1:12–20: Jesus, the "firstborn of every creature," and "all things" in him, by him, and for him). It is the covenant not simply of God as creator but of God as Jehovah, the covenant God in Jesus Christ. It is the covenant established on the basis of the sacrifice of Jesus Christ.

The establishment of the covenant as recorded in Genesis 9 is the continuation of the history of Genesis 8:20–22. It is the LORD (Jehovah) who establishes this covenant (vv. 20–21). The basis in righteousness of the covenant is the sacrifice of Noah, which typified the sacrifice of the cross (vv. 20–22).

14. Kuyper wrote many other books besides his work on common grace. Are there any works of Kuyper that you would recommend to the Reformed community to study and be excited about?

I gave the answer to this question in the April 2014 issue of the *Protestant Reformed Theological Journal* as part of my review of the fine biography of Kuyper by James D. Bratt.[30] There I recommended several of Kuyper's works in the Dutch language, including his book on the covenants (*De Leer der Verbonden*); his four-volume commentary on the Heidelberg Catechism (*E Voto Dordraceno*); and his five thick volumes of dogmatics (*Dictaten Dogmatiek*). Works of Kuyper available in English translation that I recommended included *Particular Grace* (Reformed Free Publishing Association, 2001); *When Thou Sittest in Thine House* (Eerdmans, 1929); *In the Shadow of Death* (Eerdmans, 1929; repr. Old Paths, 1994); and *To Be Near Unto God* (Eerdmans, 1918; published anew as "adapted for contemporary Christians" by Eerdmans, 1997).

15. Compare and contrast—if there is a contrast—"common" grace and "general" grace.

Kuyper himself took note of the difference between "common grace" and "general grace" in the thinking of Reformed people and often in theology. "General" grace is often understood as a universalizing of God's saving grace. Therefore, Kuyper deliberately refrained from calling the common grace he was advocating "general grace."

> We have purposely avoided the expression *general grace*, and for our title we have chosen instead *common grace*...to prevent misunderstanding. The assumption could so easily have slipped in that once again we meant [to suggest] that grace...belonged to everyone and were thereby attempting again to dislodge the established foundation of *particular* grace. The notion of "general" grace...is so easily misused, as if by it were meant *saving* grace, and that is absolutely *not* the case.[31]

In order to avoid the supposition that his doctrine of common grace was the Pelagian and Arminian universalizing

---

30 *Protestant Reformed Theological Journal* 47, no. 2 (111–29).

31 Kuyper, *Common Grace: Noah–Adam*, 11; emphasis is Kuyper's.

of saving grace, Kuyper also deliberately employed a distinctive word in Dutch for the grace that he was setting forth as common. Deliberately he described his common grace as *gratie* rather than as *genade*. The latter is the usual Dutch word for the saving grace of God. The point both of the word *gemeene* ("common") and of the word *gratie* (non-saving "grace") was sharply to distinguish cultural common grace, which is common to all humans, from saving grace (*genade*), which for Kuyper is particular, to the elect only.

It was inexcusable, therefore, that the leading theologians of the Christian Reformed Church, including Louis Berkhof, developed Kuyper's common grace (*gemeene gratie*) into Arminian, general, saving grace (*algemeene genade*), as they did in the first point of common grace. When they made Kuyper's common grace the basis of their well-meant offer of salvation, they were doing exactly what Kuyper himself warned against doing. It is even less excusable that, ninety years after the Christian Reformed synod of 1924, the Christian Reformed Church refuses to acknowledge this grievous, un-Kuyperian error of the first point of common grace, that it made general grace out of Kuyper's common grace.

The entire Reformed community of theologians shares in the fault of winking at this serious theological error, to say nothing of the doctrinal implication of the error. Where is the public recognition that the well-meant offer, apart from all other considerations, is a wholly and obviously illicit development of the common grace of Kuyper—the very error against which he explicitly warned in his books on common grace? Kuyper taught a common *non-saving, cultural* grace. He confessed that God's saving grace, both regarding the divine favor and regarding the divine power, is *particular*, condemning any extension of saving grace outside the sphere of election. Yet the Christian Reformed Church and the rest of the Reformed and Presbyterian community of churches holding the well-meant offer are the genuine disciples of Kuyper, we are told, whereas the Protestant Reformed Churches, who confess particular, saving grace, are dismissed as outside the fold of the heirs of the Dutch Reformed theologian.

But the graver issue in the matter is the reality, which history has proved, that any and all extension of the grace of God beyond Jesus Christ and the church of election inevitably results in a doctrine of a universal, saving, but ineffectual grace of God—the heresy of Arminianism, which the Reformed churches condemn in the Canons of Dordt as "altogether Pelagian and contrary to the whole Scripture."[32]

No word games can prevent it.

16. Since marriage is the most intimate union of all human relationships, does common grace then imply that believers may, should, or even ought to marry unbelievers to accomplish its goal of Christianizing society?

I doubt that even the most enthusiastic advocate of the Christianizing of the world by common grace would explicitly exhort his children or his parishioners to marry ungodly persons in order to transform and redeem society and the world.

But I have no doubt that the effect of the doctrine and practice of common grace in churches that proclaim the false doctrine is that the young people more freely date and marry ungodly and unbelieving young people of the world. If the young people of the church and the young people of the world share a grace of God, they have good, *spiritual* reason for the friendship of courting and for the union of marriage. When a young man who is a member of a Reformed church is strongly attracted to the beautiful face, shapely figure, and lively personality of an ungodly young woman, knowledge that she shares a grace of God with him is enough to bridge the gap of faith and unbelief.

In addition, the theory of common grace is the breakdown of the antithesis, which constitutes the spiritual separation of godly young people from ungodly young people and which is the ground of the prohibition against covenant young people's

---

32 Canons 3–4, Error 7, in *Confessions and Church Order*, 172.

dating worldly young people. Invariably, one of the first and most serious evidences of the breakdown of the antithesis in a church is mixed marriage, that is, the marriage of believer and unbeliever. Where common grace flourishes, one may expect the evil described in Genesis 6:2: "The sons of God saw the daughters of men that they were fair; and they took them wives of all which they chose."

I am also sure that the consequences of these mixed marriages in the churches that enthusiastically preach common grace are not at all the Christianizing of society, or even its improvement naturally. Rather, the consequences are the falling away from the Reformed churches of their young people; marital discord; divorce and remarriage; and the emotional and spiritual injuries that such a state of marital affairs effects upon the children. Although this is not the worst of the consequences of common grace and the mixed marriages that common grace encourages, mixed marriages, with their effects in divorces and broken homes, are detrimental to civil society.

In contrast, the solid marriages and homes of those who marry in the Lord, because church and parents exhort marrying only in the Lord on the basis of the doctrine of particular grace, are good for civil society. Particular grace is advantageous not only regarding the kingdom of Christ, but also regarding the earthly kingdom of nation and civil society. In the words of the apostle, "Godliness is profitable unto all things, having promise of the life that now is, and of that which is to come" (1 Tim. 4:8).

17. To your knowledge, what was the relation of church and state in Kuyper's thinking? Although he led a separation from the state church, is it possible that he believed church reformation could not be truly complete without also reforming (or Christianizing) the institution of civil government?

The question of the relation of church and state is a vexed one for all theologians.

Kuyper finally resolved, or thought to resolve, this issue by his doctrine of "sphere sovereignty." Although his view of the relation of church and state changed and developed over the years, Kuyper's mature thought on the matter was that the state is sovereign in its sphere, without encroachment by the church, and that the church is sovereign in its sphere, without encroachment by the state.

Kuyper fought for the freedom of the church from state control or influence. This was an important aspect of his struggle for reformation of the then-state church in the second half of the nineteenth century. The church is an institution of God, answerable only to God, not to the state. As Kuyper said in his lecture on "Calvinism and Politics" at Princeton Theological Seminary in 1898, "Calvinism protests against State-omnipotence; against the horrible conception that no right exists above and beyond existing laws; and against the pride of absolutism, which recognizes no constitutional rights, except as the result of princely favor."[33]

Reformed churches in the United States in 2016 do well to take Kuyper's warning against "State-omnipotence" to heart. In its assertion of its godlike omnipotence, the state decrees that unnatural, perverse sodomy and lesbianism are a form of holy marriage and then coerces submission to its lawless decree by the threat of punishment.

Kuyper saw the state as "an instrument of 'common grace,' to thwart all license and outrage and to shield the good against the evil" and also to "preserve the glorious work of God, in the creation of humanity, from total destruction."[34]

The state is not authorized by God, who is sovereign over all, to determine or interfere with the mission of the church. Neither is the church called or authorized by God to control the state, to interfere in the affairs of state, or to enlist the

---

33 Kuyper, *Lectures on Calvinism*, 98.

34 Ibid., 82–83.

sword power of the state on behalf of the establishment of one church as the church of the nation. The state is sovereign, under God, only in its own sphere. In fact, it was Kuyper and his allies who took issue with the claim of the original version of article 36 of the Belgic Confession, that the office of the magistrates includes removing and preventing all idolatry and false worship; "that the kingdom of antichrist may be thus destroyed, and the kingdom of Christ promoted."[35]

The footnote to article 36, qualifying the article for Reformed churches to this day, denies "the principle of state domination over the church," affirms "the separation of church and state," repudiates "the idea of the established church," and advocates "the autonomy of the churches and personal liberty of conscience in matters pertaining to the service of God."[36] This footnote has its origin in the thinking of Kuyper and his colleagues. A synod of the Reformed Churches in the Netherlands adopted this qualifying footnote in 1905.

The Christian Reformed Church made Kuyper's viewpoint and the qualifying footnote to article 36 their own in 1910, rejecting the notion of a "State Church." The synodical decision of the Christian Reformed Church warns against the church's or the state's encroachment "upon each other's territory," adding that "The Church has rights of sovereignty in its own sphere as well as the State."[37]

Kuyper did testify to the state and to all the society of the Netherlands that the state must recognize that it owes its authority to the sovereign God and that it must serve him. Kuyper, always very much aware of the spirit of the age, vigorously entered the lists against two powerful theories of his day concerning the state. One was that the state is absolutely sovereign as the organ of the combination of

---

35 Schaff, *Creeds of Christendom*, 3:432.

36 *Confessions and Church Order*, 74.

37 See *Acta der Synode van de Christelijke Gereformeerde Kerk, 1910* [Acts of synod of the Christian Reformed Church, 1910], 9, 104–5.

sovereign individuals. This was the theory at the heart of the French Revolution. The other theory was that the state is a mystical entity in its own right, possessing and exercising absolute power over the citizens of a nation, answerable to nothing and no one, least of all a Christian God. This theory of government, or the state, had its origin in the philosophy of the German G. F. W. Hegel. This view of the state virtually identifies the state as god.

Developments in the United States at the beginning of the twenty-first century demand that Reformed churches know and proclaim publicly, as they have opportunity, that the state owes its sovereignty to the triune God revealed in the Bible and that the state does not possess absolute sovereignty over its citizens. Then in a non-revolutionary manner, as the situation demands, the churches and their members must witness to their confession by refusing the decrees and laws of the state that contravene the laws of God both in nature and in the Bible. There soon comes again for Reformed Christians the conditions forced upon them by an antichristian state, which usurps the prerogatives of Deity, that require Christians to declare, "We ought to obey God rather than men" (Acts 5:29). Then we must suffer the consequences, as suffering persecution for God's sake.

Although the qualifying footnote to article 36 of the Belgic Confession speaks of the separation of church and state, Kuyper would not have given blanket approval to this language. He thought the church should influence the state. This influence is the calling not of the church *institute* but of the church *organism*. The church *organism* in Kuyper's theology is the lives and witness of the members of the church, as members of the one, spiritual, universal, invisible body of Christ.

Christians living a holy, God-centered life in the nation and in the society of the nation bring their Christian influence to bear also on the state, "indirectly." This influence tends to Christianize the state by the power of the common grace of God. "By its influence on the state and civil society the church of Christ aims only at a *moral triumph*, not at the imposition of confessional bonds nor at the exercise of authoritarian control."[38] It is generally acknowledged that Kuyper is the source of the distinction between the church institute and the church organism and that he came up with the distinction in the interests of the church's influencing state and society, while keeping the instituted church out of these worldly matters.

18. How did Kuyper explain the curse on Canaan in light of the theory of common grace?

Kuyper was seriously mistaken regarding the curse of Canaan, as recorded in Genesis 9:25–27, and in more than one respect. First, he explained the curse as Noah's curse upon his son Ham. This led Kuyper to judge Ham a reprobate. Thus Kuyper was able to deny that the salvation of Noah and his family in the ark was a spiritual salvation by the particular grace of God in Jesus Christ, for one of those saved was Ham, who was a reprobate in Kuyper's judgment. Reprobates are not the object of the particular, saving grace of God. The salvation in the ark therefore had to be a merely physical preservation of Noah and his family from the merely physical destruction of an earthly calamity.

Kuyper's reasoning was sound, if indeed Ham was a reprobate. But his premise was mistaken. Ham was not a reprobate. Ham was an elect child of God, who sinned grievously after leaving the ark, as did Noah himself. "Eight souls were saved by water" in the ark (1 Pet. 3:20). Noah did not curse Ham. Noah cursed Canaan.

The second mistake of Kuyper regarding the cursing of Canaan was to explain it as merely the withholding from Canaan (Ham himself, in the thinking of Kuyper) of the benefits of common grace to some extent. Canaan's descendants, who were, according to Kuyper, the black race, suffered a diminution of cultural abilities, so that they languished culturally and socially, whereas the other sons of Noah

---

38 Kuyper, "Common Grace," in Bratt, *Abraham Kuyper: A Centennial Reader*, 197.

produced the world's culture and themselves enjoyed the rich benefits of the culture of common grace: "the disappointing experience with the Negro."[39] This racial bias, as it is viewed, of Kuyper taxes his common grace disciples sorely, much more sorely than does his doctrinal error.

But Kuyper was mistaken regarding this aspect of the curse of Ham (as Kuyper insisted on viewing the curse of Canaan) also. The curse was not cultural—the cultural ineptness of the black race. The curse (of Canaan) was spiritual. The descendants of Canaan, the Canaanites, were excluded from the covenant and its salvation. In the Old Testament they were the idolatrous inhabitants of the land of Canaan before the arrival of the children of Shem. God destroyed them from before the children of Shem—the nation of Israel. The few who remained in the land of Canaan were slaves of the Israelites.

Concerning the nature and severity of the curse of Canaan, Calvin correctly speaks of separation "from the Church of God." He regards Canaan as a "reprobate" child. The effect of the curse was to deprive Canaan "of his [God's] Spirit" and to devote "the Canaanites to destruction."[40]

One thing is indisputably clear from the biblical account of the curse of Canaan and its fulfillment. There was no common grace mitigation of the curse of Canaan. Canaan and the Canaanites were fully under the curse of God. Upon them rested the divine word of malediction, bringing upon them evil in the wrath of God, and evil only. The historical realization of that word of wrath and damnation was the utter destruction of the Canaanites in the days of Joshua. Such was the determination of the Lord to destroy Canaan in fulfillment of his reprobation of Canaan, extending to his descendants, that he hardened the hearts of the Canaanites in the time of Joshua, "that they should come against Israel in battle, that he might destroy them utterly, and that they

---

39 Kuyper, *Common Grace: Noah–Adam*, 116.

40 John Calvin, *Commentaries on the First Book of Moses called Genesis*, 1:304-7.

might have no favour, but that he might destroy them, as the LORD commanded Moses" (Josh. 11:20).

19. How would you advise parents of students considering a Christian liberal arts college education?

This question is personal, not doctrinal. The question allows for, indeed requests, an answer that is subjective.

The question asks about *my* advice, my *advice*. Others may advise differently. I answer for myself.

The time was when I would have, and did, advise members of churches of which I was pastor that they should send their college students to Reformed, Christian colleges. Since Protestant Reformed parents and church members did not have, and still do not have, a college founded on and faithful to Protestant Reformed, that is, soundly Reformed, creedal principles, such a college would have been a college associated with the Christian Reformed Church or the Reformed Church in America. My advice, I supposed, was in harmony with article 21 of the Church Order of Dordt: "The consistories shall see to it that there are good Christian schools in which the parents have their children instructed according to the demands of the covenant."[41] The covenant of God with the children of believers demands that Reformed parents exert themselves to have their children instructed in good Christian schools. Since there is no Protestant Reformed college, Protestant Reformed parents and young people should use the best Christian college available.

This advice was given, of course, in the face—the *imposing* face—of the high tuition bill at a Christian college in contrast to the much cheaper cost of attending a local state college.

My family practiced what I preached. Two of our children graduated from Calvin College in Grand Rapids, Michigan. Another graduated from the basically Christian Reformed Trinity College in Palos Heights, Illinois. A fourth graduated from (Reformed) Hope College in Holland, Michigan.

---

41 *Confessions and Church Order*, 387.

I no longer urge Protestant Reformed young people to attend the Christian Reformed and Reformed colleges. If we had a child of college age, I very much doubt that my wife and I would send the child to one of these colleges or encourage him or her to attend.

The reason is not at all some characteristic Protestant Reformed animus against a Christian Reformed institution. I am deeply indebted to the education I received at Calvin College from 1956 to 1960. I openly acknowledge this indebtedness whenever doing so is appropriate, sometimes in circles where this acknowledgment does not find favor. When I was nearing graduation, I made a point of expressing my appreciation to my professors and to the administration of Calvin College for Calvin College's opening up to me the riches of learning and guiding me in becoming whatever I am of a student. I remember William Harry Jellema, John Timmerman, William Radius, Charles Miller, Walter Lagerwey, John De Vries, Robert Otten, Henry Van Til, Clifton Orlebeke, and others too many to mention.

But when a Christian college has spiritually apostatized to the degree that the biblical doctrine of creation is compromised by an evolutionary theory of origins and that there is advocacy, and even open celebration annually, of sodomy and lesbianism, when a nominally Christian college cannot condemn such heresy and perversity in uncompromising fashion and expel them unceremoniously from the sacred precincts of Reformed higher education, then I think myself permitted by God himself to turn my covenantal back on and close my covenantal wallet to such an institution. This particular unbelief and this specific depravity are not the only reasons for the rejection. These are appalling symptoms of a general, widespread, deeply rooted, fatal apostasy from the word of God, as summarized in the Reformed confessions, which is and must be the foundation and the light of all education that is Reformed and Christian.

Why spend $25,000 a year for the same instruction that can be obtained much more cheaply in a state college? Indeed, there is likely less spiritual danger for the covenant young man or woman in a state school. There the lie of evolution and the perversity of homosexuality come bold faced, undisguised, and openly anti-Christian. Against this, the Protestant Reformed young person is, or should be, on his or her guard, already at eighteen.

In a nominally Reformed college, the same falsehood and evil come cloaked in the guise of a tolerant, loving Christianity, "loving Christianity" being the popular, effective euphemism for the craven, compromising, compromised, and corrupted Christianity of our day. The latter is far more dangerous to the impressionable college student. Does God call Reformed parents to help pay $25,000 a year for the spiritual and moral seduction of their children? Not in my judgment.

This question about the college education of our young people is very much an integral part of the subject of the lecture on Kuyper's theory of cultural common grace. Kuyper's cultural common grace breaks down the antithesis—the spiritual, intellectual, and moral separation—between the church and the world. The result is that the world's thinking and the world's behavior flow into the church and her schools, as the ocean flows into the Netherlands when the dikes are breached.

Common grace has not empowered the Christian Reformed Church's Calvin College to Christianize the world. The opposite is true. Common grace has enfeebled Calvin College to the degree that it is now open to the very worst of the world's attacks on the Christian faith and scandalous corruptions of the Christian life: evolution and sexual perversity.

By 2016, it is evident to everyone that the heralding of common grace as the Christianizing of the world is empty rhetoric, laughable, if it were not so tragic in its consequences. Common grace is not the Christianizing of the world, or even of Grand Rapids, Michigan. On the contrary, common grace is the "world-izing" of Christianity in the lives, schools, and churches where this grace is taught and practiced. This is the very nature of the theory, as Hoeksema contended in 1924.

History has put the exclamation point behind his assertion.

What the Reformed community of churches and parents needs today is a soundly Reformed college, a college free from Kuyper's and the Christian Reformed Church's theory of common grace, a college truly and unashamedly based on the Reformed confessions, a college that is in reality, if not in name, Protestant Reformed.

20. How is it explained that common grace (favor) was shown to the wicked of Noah's day?

Kuyper's explanation was that in Noah and his sons was represented the entire human race, elect and reprobate, saved and unsaved, idolatrous Babylon as well as godly Judah, Emperor Nero as well as the Christians whom he would burn as torches in his gardens, Adolf Hitler as well as the Christian pastors who defied Hitler's deification of himself and suffered for it.

Salvation for Noah and his family in the ark was merely God's sparing them from physical death in the waters of the flood by his common grace. Sparing them, God spared all the members of the human race from the destruction of the flood. After the flood, by his covenant of common grace, as recorded in Genesis 9, God promised to spare all humans from a similar worldwide calamity by his common grace. Included in this promise, according to Kuyper, was God's work of restraining sin in humans and of enabling the race to develop culturally. Thus the flood, which was the awful agent of the dreadful wrath of God against the world of ungodly men and women, as ought to be evident even to the meanest intelligence on the most superficial reading of the text, becomes instead an event of common grace to the wicked.

I have already explained the covenant of Genesis 9 as a form of the covenant of particular grace in Jesus Christ.

The flood itself was divine wrath upon the workers of iniquity who had filled the cup of their rebellion and depravity. It was not only physical death to the multitudes outside the ark. It was also damnation. Such is the description of the flood in the Genesis account. Because of man's wickedness, God destroyed man in his righteous anger (Gen. 6:5–7). Such is the analysis of the flood in 2 Peter 2. The "damnation" of the wicked in the present was prefigured in the Old Testament by God's "bringing in the flood upon the world of the ungodly" (vv. 3, 5).

There was no grace in the flood for those outside the ark. There was only divine wrath, and it was terrible. There was no hint of grace in the flood for those who are outside the church of Jesus Christ. There is only the forecasting of damning wrath in the coming destruction of the world by fire (see 2 Pet. 3).

Only Noah "found grace in the eyes of the LORD" (Gen. 6:8). God's particular grace always being covenantal, this grace extended to Noah's family. Eight souls, only a "few," were graciously saved by the water of the flood (1 Pet. 3:20).

To take from the account of the flood the consoling message that God is gracious to all humans, regardless that they are not in Jesus Christ by faith in him and regardless that they live wicked lives, is to turn the biblical message of the flood on its head. Nor do we read, or have any reason to believe, that splendid cultural artifacts survived the flood. All the cultural works of the ungodly world perished with the ungodly in the raging waters of the universal flood. "The world that then was, being overflowed with water, perished" (2 Pet. 3:6).

The gospel truth of the flood, which the faithful church must proclaim both to her own members and to all those who come within hearing, is, "The heavens and the earth, which are now, by the same word are kept in store, reserved unto fire against the day of judgment and perdition of ungodly men" (2 Pet. 3:7).

Only in the church is there grace and salvation.

21. If the calling of the church is not to Christianize the world, what in a nutshell is the calling of the church given to her by Jesus Christ?

In a (biblical) nutshell, the following:

"Hold the traditions" (2 Thess. 2:15).

"Take heed...unto the doctrine" (1 Tim. 4:16).

"Earnestly contend for the faith" (Jude 3).

"Preach the word...[of] sound doctrine" (to the congregation) (2 Tim. 4:1–3).

Stop the mouths of the heretics (Titus 1:9–16).

"Teach all nations" (Matt. 28:19–20).

Keep yourself "unspotted from the world" (James 1:27).

22. Herman Hoeksema in early articles in the Banner *of 1918-1922, in the rubric "Our Doctrine," wrote frequently about amalgamation. Amalgamation, he said, was wrong. What did he mean, do you think, about his opposition to amalgamation? Is amalgamation totally the result of the theory of common grace? Can it also be man's worldly mindedness that is the cause of this amalgamation? What about amalgamation before the development of common grace?*

Hoeksema's articles in the Christian Reformed magazine the *Banner* in the early 1920s were part of the controversy in the Christian Reformed Church over the relation of church and the world, whether conformity or antithesis, leading up to the Christian Reformed Church's resolution of the controversy by the three points of common grace of 1924. Especially Professor Ralph Janssen and his supporters appealed to the theory of common grace in support of Janssen's higher critical views of the Bible (which views were conformity of Christian scholarly and doctrinal teachings to the thinking of the unbelieving world) and against the condemnation of these views by Hoeksema and others.

By "amalgamation" of the church with the world, against which he warned, Hoeksema meant the very same evil that he later described as the conformity of the church to the world. Amalgamation is the breaching or bridging of the antithesis—the spiritual separation of the church and the world.

Although the Christian Reformed theory of common grace justifies and increases amalgamation, it is not the only cause of amalgamation. Indeed, in the history of the Christian Reformed Church common grace was not the cause of amalgamation at all. On the contrary, amalgamation was the cause of the theory of common grace. There was in the Christian Reformed Church, at her highest theological levels as well as among many of the members, the burning desire to be one with the world of the ungodly—one in her thinking and one in her behavior. There was love of the world and desire for friendship with the world. The world was attractive.

Separation from that lovely world, much more enmity with that lovely world, seemed embarrassing, provincial, isolationist, Anabaptist. The world beckoned with all the seductive power of the heathen nations upon Israel in the Old Testament, of Delilah upon Samson, of the world of the epistles of John upon the New Testament church. Antithetical separation seemed to deprive the church of standing and reputation in the world; of delightful pleasures, intellectual as well as moral, that the world offered; and yes, of the possibility of influencing the world.

The Christian Reformed Church seized upon the theology of common grace as the doctrinal basis of the amalgamation she so eagerly desired. Since no less a Reformed figure than Kuyper had recently spun out of his political, cultural, world-influencing soul the theory of common grace, common grace could function powerfully as the *Reformed* theological basis of amalgamation. Opponents of amalgamation, especially Hoeksema, could be defeated not only as those standing in the way of the amalgamation for which the Christian Reformed Church lusted, but also as un-Reformed. The theory of common grace served the fundamental error of world conformity.

Man's worldly mindedness is indeed the explanation of amalgamation. Man's worldly mindedness is love of the ungodly world rather than love of God, which love of God is hatred of the ungodly world with all its works and ways. "Ye adulterers and adulteresses, know ye not that the friendship of the world is enmity with God? whosoever therefore will be a friend of the world is the enemy of God" (James 4:4).

Implied is that although rejection of common grace hinders the evil of world conformity in churches that condemn the false doctrine and although rejection of common grace is testimony to the antithesis and its essential importance, a church can become worldly even though she denies common grace. Certainly the lives of members of churches that deny common grace can succumb to the temptation of worldliness. Certainly the powerful temptation of worldliness of thinking and behavior is a threat to us all, including the most vigorous theological opponent of common grace.

The seven churches of Asia Minor, addressed in Revelation 2 and 3, had not been corrupted by a theory of common grace. But many of them were yielding in various ways to the temptation of conforming to the wicked world around them.

23. Herman Hoeksema spoke enthusiastically that people need to be more concerned and enthusiastic in the cosmological salvation rather than merely a personal salvation. Did he not in a sense receive support for this from Abraham Kuyper?

I wish that this questioner had referenced the enthusiasm of Hoeksema for cosmological salvation, so that I could check out the context of this enthusiasm.

That Hoeksema taught God's salvation of the created world and not only of humans is beyond question. His correction of the common explanation of John 3:16, as though the text teaches a love of God for all humans without exception, rightly called attention to the truth that the text teaches God's love for the created universe (Greek: *kosmos*) with its various creatures, non-human as well as human.

Hoeksema taught that the human objects of the particular, saving grace of God in Jesus Christ are all nations and peoples *in the elect among them*. Hoeksema also taught that God's salvation of humans is such a power as to extend to all aspects of the lives of these humans—family, education, work, personal relationships, and more. Are these the enthusiasm for cosmological salvation to which the questioner refers?

Hoeksema may very well have been influenced in these respects, as he certainly was influenced in other theological respects, by Kuyper. Hoeksema did not reject Kuyper. He rejected Kuyper's theory of common grace.

Much as I share this enthusiasm for cosmological salvation as outlined above, I hesitate to describe zeal for personal salvation as "merely." There is nothing "mere" about personal salvation. Only with great effort, if at all, can I be enthusiastic about the salvation of the *kosmos* apart from my gratitude and joy over the salvation of myself personally and of the church of fellow believers and their children.

24. The Christian Reformed Church during their controversy over common grace in the 1920s did not see it necessary to translate Abraham Kuyper's Common Grace. *What purpose does the recent translation of this work serve? Why now? Is there a relationship between its current translation and the doctrine of the federal vision?*

In 1924 many in the Christian Reformed Church, including a majority of ministers, could read Dutch. There was no need, therefore, to translate the work into English. Today the vast majority of ministers and professors committed to Kuyper's theory of common grace, not only in the Christian Reformed Church, but also in the United Reformed Churches and other Reformed and Presbyterian churches, are unable to read Dutch. For them, it is necessary that the fountainhead of their theory of common grace be translated into English.

The purpose of the present translation of Kuyper's work on common grace into English is, in general, the revival and spread of the theory of cultural common grace, as well as stimulation of the zeal of Reformed people on behalf of the implementation of the theory, namely, the effort to Christianize North America and then the whole world.

The purpose of the project, in particular, is that Kuyper's work on common grace may serve today as the basis of the cooperation of Reformed people and Roman Catholics in the great work of Christianizing the world. Supporters of the project and its practical purpose would say that there is great need today for the cooperation of Rome and the Reformed in fighting the culture wars because of the aggression of the ungodly in making the culture antichristian, for example, in the promotion of sodomy and lesbianism.

In addition to the fact that the Bible nowhere calls the church or Christians to Christianize the world, as well as the fact that the theory of common grace is a weak weapon with which to withstand the assaults of the world and to defeat this enemy (take note of the real and mighty weapons of the Christian in his warfare with the world in Ephesians 6!), cooperation of Reformed people with Rome in any spiritual endeavor whatsoever reminds me of the fable of the spider and the fly. "Come into my parlor, said the (Roman Catholic) spider to the (Reformed) fly!"

Rome has no love for the Reformed faith, as her decrees of the Council of Trent make plain. Rome is as much an enemy of the Reformed faith and church as is the world. The result of foolish cooperation on the part of Reformed theologians and churches with Rome in this or any other spiritual enterprise will be that Rome will devour the Reformed. This has already begun to happen in that the Christian Reformed Church has reduced question 80 of the Heidelberg Catechism, *the* anti-Roman Catholic article in the catechism and therefore *the* defense of Reformed Christianity against Rome, to an insignificant footnote.

The book of Revelation prophesies that the warfare of the true church of Jesus Christ at the end—the time in which we live—will be against the beast from the sea (the world of ungodly nations and governments united under one head) in league with the beast from the earth (the false church, of which Rome is the main protagonist). See Revelation 13.

The reference in this question to the heresy of the federal vision has merit. The conditional theology of the federal vision is essentially the Roman Catholic doctrine of salvation: justification by faith and by good works. That reunion with Rome is in the mind of the advocates of the federal vision is evident in Norman Shepherd's declaration that his doctrine of justification by faith and works offers "hope for a common understanding between Roman Catholicism and evangelical Protestantism regarding the way of salvation."[42] Shepherd, of course, is a leading proponent, if not the father, of the theology of the federal vision.

In addition, the main proponents of the theology of the federal vision, Shepherd and the Christian Reconstructionists, are postmillennialists. They look for an earthly kingdom of Christ in history. The enthusiastic advocates of common grace, now busy in cooperating in the translation of Kuyper's work on common grace, entertain the postmillennial dream of Christianizing North America and then the world with the help of Rome. The men of the federal vision share the postmillennial dream.

25. What incentive did and do Roman Catholics have to adopt this theory of common grace as their motive to cooperation, since it refuses to recognize them as the objects of particular grace?

By their cooperation with Reformed theologians in translating and promoting Kuyper's work on common grace, the Roman Catholic theologians of the Acton Institute do not necessarily "adopt" the theory of common grace. But these astute Roman Catholic thinkers do *recognize* Kuyper's theory of common grace as essentially Roman Catholic doctrine. Rome has always taught that God has a love or favor for all humans

---

42 Norman Shepherd, *The Call of Grace: How the Covenant Illuminates Salvation and Evangelism* (Phillipsburg, NJ: P&R, 2000), 59.

without exception. Rome has always taught that the fall of the human race in Adam left fallen humans with a residue of good, with the ability to please God in everyday, natural life, and that this preservation of the race from a condition of total depravity is due to a love, or favor, or grace of God toward all without exception. Whether one calls this grace common or special is of no importance to Rome. Rome's thinking is that grace is grace, so that even if Reformed thinkers, like Kuyper, hesitate at first to describe this grace as special and saving, eventually they will come around to viewing it as also a saving grace.

Rome is right. The Christian Reformed Church proved Rome right in 1924 when it described the common grace that it was approving as including a well-meant offer of salvation to all humans. A well-meant offer is the expression not merely of a cultural common grace, but of a universal (ineffectual) saving grace of God. This is quintessential Roman Catholic doctrine.

Kuyper's theory of common grace, as developed and explained by the Christian Reformed Church, does indeed recognize Roman Catholics as objects of what this questioner describes as "particular" grace, that is, a grace that is saving in design and nature.

Rome has always had the determination to bring the whole world under the rule and influence of the Roman Catholic Church and its pope. Whatever means serve to realize this determination are acceptable to Rome, from physical weapons, to the blatant lying of the Jesuits, to a theory of common grace. All that matters is that the world is subject to Rome. Revelation 17 foretells that Rome will be successful. For a while, in the future, the great whore, who is drunken with the blood of the martyrs, will ride the scarlet beast. All who cooperate with Rome in her campaign to dominate the world, although Reformed in name, will ride the beast with Rome. This is not a good, honorable, or promising position.

The reputedly conservative Reformed men and institutions now cooperating with the Roman Catholics of the Acton Institute to Christianize North America and then the world by a common grace of God are pawns on Rome's chessboard—*willing* pawns, but pawns. These prominent pawns very likely will bring their churches into Rome's fatal embrace.

26. Please give evidence of the United Reformed Churches defending common grace as rigorously as the Christian Reformed Church. There are certainly United Reformed men and ministers who do not subscribe to common grace. Many who say they do, if asked further, will not define common grace as the Christian Reformed Church did at the Synod of Kalamazoo so many years ago.

I have proved the commitment of the United Reformed Churches to the theory of common grace, not only the cultural common grace of Kuyper, but also the theory of common grace adopted by the Christian Reformed Church in 1924, in my answer to question 10. I refer this questioner to my response to this question.

But this question provides me the opportunity to reflect further on the calling of the United Reformed Churches regarding the doctrine of common grace. If these churches repudiate the doctrine of common grace that the Christian Reformed Church adopted in 1924, let them say so openly, publicly, and by synodical decision. At the very least, let their leading spokesmen, the theologians of Mid-America and Westminster West, say so.

There is no such repudiation of the doctrine of common grace either by the federation or by its leading theologians. Much less is there any public acknowledgment of the righteous cause of the Protestant Reformed Churches in proclaiming particular, sovereign grace. The leading theologians of the United Reformed Churches are as dismissive of the Protestant Reformed Churches and contemptuous of their theology as any of the fiercest enemies of the Protestant Reformed Churches in the Christian Reformed Church.

If theologians in the United Reformed Churches reject common grace, they do so privately, safely whispering their disagreement to a close circle of friends. After all the long and well-known history of the controversy over common grace between the Protestant Reformed Churches and the Christian Reformed Church and in view of the abuse of the Protestant Reformed Churches by the Christian Reformed Church over the issue of common grace, for those who for years were part of the Christian Reformed Church and therefore fully responsible for the common grace decisions of the Christian Reformed Church, as well as for the abuse of the Protestant Reformed Churches for rejecting common grace—I say, for those men merely privately to whisper their rejection of common grace among themselves is dishonorable. Mere ecclesiastical honorableness requires that they speak out openly, before the Reformed church world.

In striking contrast to the United Reformed Churches, leading Christian Reformed theologians today are open in charging injustice by the Christian Reformed Church in its treatment of Hoeksema and in questioning at least the creedal Reformed character of the Christian Reformed Church's three points of common grace of 1924, if not the doctrine itself. One has brought an overture on these matters to the synod of the Christian Reformed Church. This is honorable behavior.

Where are such public statements on these issues by the men of the United Reformed Churches?

The United Reformed Churches as a federation of churches represents objection to one of the fruits and consequences of the Christian Reformed Church's doctrine of common grace, for which it, as essentially nothing more than the Christian Reformed Church without women in office, is fully responsible before God and the churches. It is not and has never claimed to be a genuine, principled, radical (that is, getting at the root of heresies) reformation of the Christian Reformed Church as a church that embraced both Kuyperian, world-conforming common grace and Arminian, universal, ineffectual saving grace (the well-meant offer) in that church's adoption of the three points of common grace of 1924.

This is what the leading men of the United Reformed Churches ought to have done at the very beginning of their movement and what the United Reformed Churches are called to do still today: confess the sin of the Christian Reformed Church, of which they were still a part at the beginning of their movement, in adopting the false doctrine of the three points of common grace of 1924 and the grievous sin of deposing from office sound, Reformed ministers of the word and soundly Reformed consistories of elders and deacons on the ground, in reality, of their refusing to corrupt the doctrines of the Canons of Dordt. Sensitive consciences would have added the sin of blackening and slandering the Protestant Reformed Churches before the entire Reformed church world for many years for no other reason, in reality, than that these churches do wholeheartedly preach, confess, *and defend* the doctrines of the Canons of Dordt. The synod of the Christian Reformed Church that adopted the three points of common grace in 1924 acknowledged that Hoeksema and his colleagues were soundly Reformed according to the Reformed confessions.

Then the leading men of the United Reformed Churches ought to have asked themselves, in the presence of God, whether there is any reason for the existence of yet another Reformed federation alongside the Protestant Reformed denomination; whether the true unity of the church, about which the United Reformed Churches make a lot of noise, does not require them to seek admission to or union with the Protestant Reformed Churches; whether establishing yet another Reformed federation does not, in fact, constitute sin against the unity of the church; and whether, in addition, their adding their voice to the criticism of the Protestant Reformed Churches for confessing particular grace does not betray the United Reformed Churches for what they are in reality: the Christian Reformed Church without women in office.

About this issue of women in office, I wrote before and, despite the criticism I drew, write once again that I could easier live with a female preacher who proclaimed sovereign, particular grace than with a male preacher who preached and taught the three points of common grace of 1924 of the Christian Reformed Church and of the United Reformed Churches. I could shut my eyes to the female preacher; I could not close my ears to the message of the male Arminian masquerading as a Reformed preacher. The issue of women in ecclesiastical office pales in comparison with the issue of common grace, especially the common grace of a well-meant offer of salvation to all humans. Indeed, the former sin of practice is the fruit of the latter sin of doctrine.

(This question was submitted sometime after the lecture, evidently occasioned by the answers to previous questions that were posted on the internet.)

27. Do you believe that the doctrine of common grace has bearing on the doctrine of the covenant? Is there a connection between common grace and the federal vision heresy? Can one hold to the covenant position of Klaas Schilder without believing in common grace?

This cluster of questions concerns the relation of a theory of common grace to the biblical, Reformed doctrine of the covenant. The questions raise the hot topic in the Reformed community of churches in North America of the covenantal doctrine that calls itself the federal vision. They suggest, correctly, an intimate relationship between the federal vision and the theology of the Dutch theologian Klaas Schilder.

I will not here go into detail in grounding my response to the cluster of questions, in part to keep my response brief and in part because I have explained the covenantal doctrine of the federal vision and demonstrated its essential oneness with the theology of Schilder and of the Reformed Churches in the Netherlands ("liberated"), as well as of their daughter churches in North America (the Canadian Reformed Churches) and elsewhere. This can be found in two books, *Covenant and Election in the Reformed Tradition* (Reformed

Free Publishing Association, 2011) and *Federal Vision: Heresy at the Root* (Reformed Free Publishing Association, 2012).

Regarding the question of the bearing that common grace might have on the doctrine of the covenant, in fact the synodical decision of the Christian Reformed Church in 1924 adopting three points of common grace rather is evidence of the bearing of a certain doctrine of the covenant on the doctrine of common grace. The doctrine of the covenant that prevailed in the Christian Reformed Church in the early 1920s was that of Prof. Heyns, a professor at Calvin Theological Seminary—the seminary of the Christian Reformed Church. Heyns taught that all the baptized children of believing parents are alike included in the covenant of grace, in the sense that God loves them all, desires to save them all, and even begins a work of saving grace in them all. However, the continuation of this grace and its fulfillment in the salvation of a child are conditioned on the child's own activity of faith and obedience.

Because this covenantal doctrine of universal, conditional grace obtained in the Christian Reformed Church, the synod of 1924 could readily adopt both Kuyper's theory of a universal common (non-saving) grace and the Arminian theory of a universal saving grace (the well-meant offer). A heretical covenantal doctrine produced, or at least paved the way for, the false doctrine of common grace in the Christian Reformed Church.

In the thinking of the theologians and ministers of the Christian Reformed Church, grace does not originate in or depend upon election. For them, election is not the fountain and cause of grace, regardless of the teaching of their creed, the Canons of Dordt.

Regarding the theology of the federal vision, its teachers, who are developing and promoting the covenantal doctrine of Schilder and the liberated Reformed churches by whatever denominational name they go, are not especially advocates of Kuyper's non-saving, cultural, common grace. Rather, the federal vision teaches a *saving* grace of God for all the children of believing parents, if not for all humans without exception. I add the phrase "if not for all humans without exception" for good reason. Defenders of the covenantal theology of the federal vision, including the enormously influential Norman Shepherd, explain John 3:16 as a love of God for all humans without exception. The love of God of John 3:16 is obviously not a non-saving, cultural love or grace, but the love that gave Jesus Christ for the salvation of sinners.

The heresy of the federal vision is its doctrine of a universal, saving, but conditional (and therefore ineffectual) love or grace of God especially for all the children of believers, Esau as well as Jacob. It is a new form of the Arminian heresy exposed and condemned by the Canons of Dordt.

The federal vision, by its own open declaration, is the contemporary development and bold proclamation of the covenantal theology of Schilder and the liberated Reformed. As the federal vision makes unmistakably plain and forthrightly states to the entire Reformed church world, the covenantal doctrine of Schilder, his disciples, and their churches is a doctrine of universal, special, saving, but conditional grace. It is Arminianism with particular application to the covenant. One cannot hold the covenantal doctrine of Schilder and the liberated Reformed without embracing the false doctrine of a saving grace of God that is common to elect believers and reprobate unbelievers, common to those who are saved and to those who perish.

The doctrine of the covenant of Heyns, of the Christian Reformed Church, of Schilder and the liberated Reformed, and of the federal vision is not merely a form of Kuyperian, cultural, common grace. It is far worse. It is a form of the doctrine of universal, but conditional, *saving* grace that Kuyper condemned in his book *Dat de Genade Particulier is* (That [saving] grace is particular). This book has been translated into English by Marvin Kamps as *Particular Grace* and is available from the Reformed Free Publishing Association.

Although, as the answer to this question shows, there is an important distinction between Kuyper's common grace and the universal (saving, conditional) grace of the Arminian heresy, the truth simplifies matters. The truth is that there is one, and one only, grace of God. This grace is his particular favor in Jesus Christ, originating in God's eternal decree of election, that saves elect sinners from sin and death and empowers them to live godly lives in all areas of human, earthly life (culture).

Once this truth of particular grace in Jesus Christ, rooted in election, is compromised, the churches guilty of the compromise go wrong in all kinds of ways, invariably also by making the saving grace of God universal, conditional, and ineffectual.